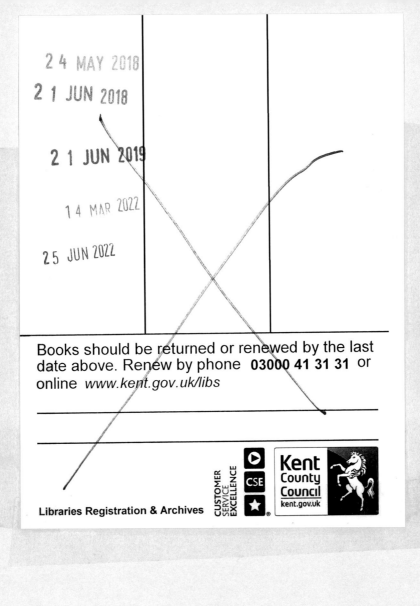

D1321156

KATE

How to Dress Like a Style Icon

THIS IS A CARLTON BOOK

This edition published in 2018
First published in 2013 by Carlton Books Limited
20 Mortimer Street
London W1T 3JW

10 9 8 7 6 5 4 3 2 1

A CIP catalogue record for this book is available from
the British Library.

ISBN: 978-1-78097-071-3

Senior Executive Editor: Lisa Dyer
Managing Art Director: Lucy Coley
Production Manager: Maria Petalidou
Copy Editor: Jane Donovan
Research Assistant: Ellen Wallwork

Printed in Dubai

Cover photographs courtesy of Getty Images,
L.K. Bennett, Libélula, Heavenly Necklaces, Anya
Hindmarch, Kiki McDonough, R.Soles & Stuart
Weitzman

KATE

How to Dress Like a Style Icon

FASHION FROM A ROYAL ROLE MODEL

CAROLINE JONES

CARLTON
BOOKS

Contents

Introduction   6

All about Kate   8

The Look Book   28

Kate's Style Directory   194

Index   204

Acknowledgements   207

Introduction

Even when she was plain old Kate, a pretty student who just happened to be dating Britain's most eligible bachelor, there was something about Miss Middleton that captured the world's imagination. Back in 2002, the 20-year-old already possessed a certain quiet poise, along with an easy smile and an indisputable eye for a striking outfit. As Catherine, Duchess of Cambridge, the fresh-faced student has now evolved into a bona fide fashion queen, with a wardrobe that inspires millions of avid followers and has spawned a thousand imitations.

Part of the fascination is of course rooted in Kate's own history. The daughter of two former British Airways flight attendants, who went on to marry a prince and become a style icon, is perhaps as close to a modern-day fairytale as you can get. Her down-to-earth background has never prevented her from mingling effortlessly in elite circles, and it is this unique melting pot of lower-middle- and upper-class influences that gave birth to her signature style – a perfect blend of high-street and designer clothing. Kate has mixed everything up to create a fresh twist on classic British clothing – a look so simple yet so stylish that women across the globe want to emulate it. It has turned the Duchess into a global trend-setter, with a host of blogs and Twitter feeds dedicated solely to hunting down her latest must-have outfit.

On April 29, 2011, that outfit was an incomparable Sarah Burton for Alexander McQueen wedding dress, but it's perhaps the clever choices she has made since that show-stopping day that have done more to cement Kate's fashion-leader credentials. In recent years, we have seen her consistently hone her personal style during a non-stop diary of official engagements – and continue to evolve her look since becoming a mother.

Particular fashion highlights have included the stunning outfits she wore for the Queen's Diamond Jubilee celebrations in 2012 and Princess Charlotte's christening in 2015, but many of her more casual looks have proved equally influential.

Selecting outfit after stunning outfit for such a variety of engagements on such a public stage is an enormously tricky task but one that Kate pulls off with aplomb and without the assistance of so much as a personal stylist. And if she can do all this on her own, then there's hope for the rest of us! Which is why we've created this timely book – an insider's guide that not only celebrates Kate's inspirational fashion flair but also makes it possible to steal some of her style tricks.

We begin by looking in some depth at the components of Kate's "look" and the impact it has had on both the retail and the fashion worlds. After that, the heart of the book focuses on what everyone wants to know most of all – where exactly do the Duchess's key fashion pieces come from, and how can we follow her fashion lead without having to marry a prince or go bankrupt in the process? With beautiful glossy photographs, we break down 50 of Kate's most memorable outfits, examining the shops, the designers and the history behind them.

As well as revealing Kate's personal style secrets, the text is also packed with practical tips that hold true for any budget, such as how to pick the perfect "Kate" blazer, and ways to work her favourite heels. It's everything you need to know to try and emulate perhaps the most stylish British woman of the century: Catherine, Duchess of Cambridge, aka "Kate the Great".

All about Kate

In the 15 years since she first caught Prince William's eye while wearing a see-through chiffon frock at the now infamous University of St Andrews student fashion show, Catherine, Duchess of Cambridge, has become one of the biggest British style icons in living memory. Her elegant look has sparked copycat imitations the world over and created a recession-beating boost in sales for the shops and designers whose clothes she favours. Indeed, so pronounced is the "Kate Effect" globally that, in 2012, *Time* magazine selected Kate as one of The 100 Most Influential People in the World.

Kate's sartorial superstar status was cemented a year earlier, when she was crowned the "Queen of Style" by upmarket fashion bible *Harper's Bazaar*. In topping the glossy magazine's celebrated Britain's Best Dressed list, Kate was praised for her "effortless" mix of high-end and high-street style, as well as for her role in the "fashion moment of the century" – her Sarah Burton for Alexander McQueen wedding dress. This was the making of a modern princess, played out in her fashion choices – as *Harper's* editor Lucy Yeomans noted: "Catherine's incredible style evolution has gripped us all."

RIGHT: Kate wore this glamorous floor-length coral satin dress by designer Issa to attend the Boodle Boxing Ball in aid of the Starlight Children's foundation at the Royal Lancaster Hotel London on January 7, 2008.

OPPOSITE: The Duchess wears a pretty floral dress by Jenny Packham to a charity polo match in Santa Barbara on July 9, 2011, which she attended with husband Prince William.

The Evolution of an Iconic Look

After graduating from St Andrews in 2006 with a History of Art degree, Kate worked as an accessories buyer for the high-street store Jigsaw. It was here, working behind the scenes, that she honed an ability to make classic high-street staples look like a million dollars and developed an eye for picking a simple but stunning final touch for an outfit – be it that perfect-width belt or eye-catching scarf. During her time there, Kate even collaborated with successful jewellery designer Claudia Bradby on a "coffee bean" necklace that became a bestseller.

And yet, as far back as 2002, when Kate first began dating Prince William, it was clear that the young lady knew how to dress. Despite her slightly shy public demeanour, Kate always had a firm idea of who she was, and she wasn't the type to be easily swayed by passing fashion fads.

Tall and willowy, her model-like figure has always meant she could pull off pretty much any style or shape of clothing, so it's testament to her strong sense of identity that she has chosen, by and large, to stick to a simple but effective fashion formula. The look may have been honed, sharpened and sprinkled with designer pieces over the last few years, but the fundamentals have been in place since her student days. Kate's fail-safe ensemble usually includes: knee-length shift dresses, simple court shoes and her favourite envelope-style clutch bag. These elegant shapes flatter her slender frame and have become the mainstay of her wardrobe. They also echo her character traits of loyalty, stability and quiet confidence.

The roots of Kate's look can be found in "Sloane" style – a not-always complimentary slang term used to describe the trendy upper middle-class inhabitants of expensive areas of west London, such as Chelsea and Kensington. The future Duchess may have been brought up in rural Berkshire but throughout her private schooling she mixed with the smart set, and now, as perhaps the most famous resident of west London, she is the foremost ambassador for the modern Sloane look. A typical "uniform" for a so-called Sloane Ranger includes costly country casuals such as Barbour wax jackets, navy blazers and Hunter wellies – a look worn by most members of the Royal Family, it should also be noted!

But while her trademark style is not new, what makes Kate stand apart is the fact that she has added her very own modern twists to invigorate what was essentially a tired, out-of-touch look. If Sloane style is typically safe and slow to evolve, Kate has extended it to include innovative dresses by high-fashion designers, along with a good-sized helping of high-street flourishes. This embrace of the best of the British high street has been particularly important in fostering the public's love affair with the Duchess. It's safe to say that in these financially cautious times much of the appeal of Kate's signature style is that it feels accessible as much as aspirational.

OPPOSITE AND ABOVE:
Sloane style outdoors: Kate at the Badminton Horse Trials in May 2007, opposite far left; at a game fair at Blenheim Palace in July 2004, opposite left; and attending the Golden Metropolitan Polo Club Charity Cup polo match, in which Prince William and Prince Harry played, at the Beaufort Polo Club in June 2012.

OVERLEAF: Kate in night-out-on-the-town mode, both 2007.

Another notable aspect of the look is Kate's old-fashioned take on female sexuality. With skirts never too short and heels never too high, her style has been dubbed "the new demure" but she still manages to look feminine and alluring. Less on show is certainly more, as far as she is concerned. This focused but not inflexible style is what has helped Kate assume iconic fashion status. Like any classic style idol – from Audrey Hepburn's boyish Capri pants and ballet flats chic to Gwen Stefani's rock-glamour – it's all about finding a strong look and ensuring its themes run through every outfit you choose. With Kate, this strong style core seems to come naturally as she channels her sartorial heritage with charm but manages to appear fresh and modern at the same time.

The fact that royal etiquette forbids the Duchess to accept freebies may in itself have contributed to her independent thinking. Unlike your average celebrity, Kate is not in thrall to any of the big fashion houses and simply wears clothes that she really likes. Most probably, she even looks at the price tags! Her independent streak runs deep – in this day and age, it's hard to believe that Kate has never once hired a personal stylist. Instead, she has masterminded her own fashion transformation, single-handedly shopping for all her own clothes. This brave decision shows how much the Duchess knows her own mind and is an indication that she doesn't indiscriminately choose pieces, but is making a deliberate, well-thought-out style statement.

And the personal involvement shows – despite the international stage and media masses, Kate never looks like a clothes-horse wearing some uncomfortable creation for the first time. On almost all occasions, formal and informal, she appears relaxed, self-assured and totally happy with her outfit choices. After all, this is a lady who is confident enough in her shopping skills to think nothing of popping down to Bicester Village Shopping Outlet to pick up a cut-price bargain Missoni coat for an official engagement with HM the Queen!

Although Kate still gravitates toward the mid-range high-street stores such as Whistles, L.K. Bennett and Reiss, as she has been increasingly thrust into the limelight, her style has continued to mature and evolve. With the confidence of an established public figure and as mother to a growing royal brood, the Duchess has continued to evolve her look and become increasingly daring with her outfits, choosing vibrant colours and eye-catching designs for eveningwear, such as the striking off-the-shoulder Alexander McQueen dress she wore to the BAFTAs in February 2017. Never afraid to reach for accessories to refresh her look, Kate has become an accomplished fascinator wearer, first demonstrated by the stylish tan Whiteley Hat Company creation she wore to the Epsom Derby in June 2011. Teamed with a white Reiss dress, Joseph jacket and L.K. Bennett clutch, it triggered a flurry of sales, with Debenhams department store selling seven fascinators for every hat. And, in November 2012, she decided to reinvent the carefully blow-dried long hairstyle she had sported since university days by adding a daring side fringe – a look she returned to again in 2015 following Princess Charlotte's birth.

The "Kate Effect"

It's safe to say that Kate's impact on fascinator sales wasn't a one-off. Figures from search engine Google reveal that "The Duchess of Cambridge" is one of the most searched-for fashion buzzwords, as followers desperately try to find out where her latest outfit was purchased and how they can get their hands on it. She may rarely be seen wearing something as pricey as the latest must-have Manolo Blahniks or Mulberry tiger-print bag, but the Duchess certainly has the ability to shift thousands of copies of her high-street favourites, be it a simple Zara dress or a pair of L.K. Bennett pumps.

Kate is perhaps the first style superstar of the social media age, and her effect on sales is often instantaneous as her fans immediately take to Twitter and Facebook to find out more. Numerous blogs, including What Kate Wore, and mobile apps such as Kate's Style List, have been launched to make following her fashion choices even easier. Examples of this effect are everywhere. When Kate wore a black velvet coat by Libélula to the wedding of Sarah Stourton and Harry Aubrey-Fletcher in January 2011, it sold out in hours, the company website crashed and the coat soon had a waiting list of 300.

After Kate chose to wear a Reiss "Nannette" dress for her engagement portrait by Mario Testino, astonished company founder David Reiss stated: "We have been inundated with press coverage – at one stage, online was selling one per minute." The Duchess again opted for the high-street brand when she met the Obamas at Buckingham Palace during their state visit in May 2011. Unsurprisingly, the "Shola" pale camel bandage dress she wore flew out of stores at break-neck speed. "We're really proud that Kate is a Reiss customer," said a delighted David Reiss, with some understatement. "She has the eyes of the world on her and is an incredible ambassador."

Even a low-key event can have the same effect. When Kate chose to wear a red Luisa Spagnoli suit to visit her old university, St Andrews, she caused a now-familiar shopping frenzy at Hollie de Keyser, the London boutique that stocks the label. "We re-ordered 100 suits – that's £50,000-worth (over $80,600) of stock. Since Kate wore the suit, we've been inundated," the store said.

And if customers cannot always afford the real thing, simply buying something similar will often suffice. Perhaps unsurprisingly, the famous royal blue Issa dress worn by Kate when Buckingham Palace announced the royal engagement sold out in under 24 hours. More impressively, the copycat version at Tesco was also snapped up within an hour of going online. And after Kate's £650 ($1,000) Burberry coat quickly sold out after she first wore it in March 2011, supermarket fashion brand George at Asda quickly reported a 300 per cent surge in sales of their similar cut-price mac.

Nor is Kate's fashion influence restricted to the general public. Hollywood's elite have been equally impressed by her dress sense, with actress Anne Hathaway speaking for many when she declared: "Can I tell you how grateful I am to Kate Middleton?

Because she is such an advocate for dressing like a lady."

Even for a Queen-in-waiting, Kate's impact so far on the fashion industry has been truly remarkable, already surpassing that of her style icon predecessor, Diana, Princess of Wales. The impact is now so pronounced that any brand ailing in the current economy must hope and pray that the Duchess decides to slip on one of their designs. Time and again we have seen her endorsement of British labels cause shoppers to forget economic uncertainty and spend, spend, spend! In fact, the "Kate Effect" is probably unparalleled in fashion history in terms of its impact on sales.

In 2012, the year London hosted the Olympic Games, influential American magazine *Newsweek* stated: "The Kate Effect may be worth £1 billion to the UK fashion industry." Later that year, Dr Harold Goodwin, a professor of tourism at Leeds Metropolitan University, was quoted as saying: "I wouldn't be surprised if Kate Middleton's legacy is bigger than that of the Olympics, domestically and internationally."

Unsurprisingly, since the births of Prince George and Princess Charlotte, what's now been dubbed "The Cambridge Effect" has extended to Kate's children, with a fashion frenzy around every new outfit they wear. In 2016, US *Forbes* magazine stated: "Every article of their clothing seen publicly, from a small pin in Princess Charlotte's hair to the socks sported by the little prince, become objects of utmost attraction for millions of shoppers. Like their mother, every appearance ripples through the industry and the brands that create them experience massive online traffic surges and orders."

OPPOSITE: Kate holds her own in a simple camel bandage "Shola" dress from one of her favourite brands, Reiss, while meeting the equally stylish US First Lady Michelle Obama at Buckingham Palace on May 24, 2011.

ABOVE: Kate cheers on the British Olympic team at the Women's Laser Radial race in Weymouth in August 2012, along with Princess Anne and Sir Steve Redgrave.

Pippa: It's a Sister Act

Of course, Kate isn't the only Middleton lady to hit the style headlines. Ever since younger sister Pippa stepped out of the wedding car to assist Kate down the aisle at Westminster Abbey, she's been creating some fashion waves of her own. Her stunning yet simple cream silk Alexander McQueen bridesmaid dress drew praise from around the world – much of it centred on her rather well-shaped bottom, gaining the then-27-year-old the press nickname "Her Royal Hotness".

But it's not just her derrière that has caused excitement – her sense of style has created its own "Pippa Effect" on clothes sales. This phenomenon first started when the Zara jacket she wore on her first public outing after the Royal Wedding became an instant classic. Soon after, her trusty Modalu "Bristol" bag was quickly renamed the "Pippa", and stockist John Lewis were toasting Kate's sister for helping it ride out the high-street sales slumps.

Pipbta's style, it must be said, is heavily indebted to her older sister, as demonstrated by the fact that, when she attended the wedding of Camilla Hook to Sam Holland in May 2012, she wore a red version of the same Issa "Forever" dress that Kate famously wore in her royal engagement photos. And yet, as befits a younger sister, Pippa does have a noticeable penchant for brighter colours and higher hemlines. It's a more overtly sexy style that reflects the fact she's not set to be a future queen. But like her royal sibling, Pippa continues to loudly declare her love of the British high street by stepping out in bargain dresses and jackets. When she attended the US Open Tennis Championships on her 29th birthday in September 2012, she wore a canary-yellow shift dress by Phase Eight – a mid-price, high-street brand specializing in day and formal dresses. On the same trip, she worked both a bold multicoloured block dress by London designer Paper, and a sky-blue blouse from ubiquitous high-street brand Next. Perhaps unsurprisingly, pretty soon Pippa's unofficial state visit was attracting the attention of some serious players in the US fashion world.

Fashion brand Kate Spade New York spoke for many in America when it commended Pippa on her "feminine yet modern sense of style", noting: "She always looks effortlessly put together and isn't afraid to wear colour." The same label was also impressed by Pippa's take on a great Middleton tradition: fashion recycling. "We think it's fantastic how Pippa repeats her outfits and accessories," said a spokesperson for Kate Spade. "It sets a great example that fashion doesn't have to be thrown out after one wear." With such global style recognition, little wonder Pippa was also named by *Time* magazine as one of their 100 Most Influential People of 2012 – a new entry that ousted poor Prince William from the list!

At the launch of her party book *Celebrate: A Year of British Festivities for Families and Friends*, Pippa sealed her fashion status in the eyes of the world. Ms Middleton wore no fewer

OPPOSITE AND ABOVE:
Pretty girls in pretty dresses. Kate and Pippa attend Simon Sebag Montefiore's *Young Stalin* book launch on May 14, 2007, at Aspreys, London, opposite, and the sisters walk about town in 2008, above.

than four different designer dresses over 24 hours in London – costing a total of around £3,000 ($4,800). She began her day with a visit to Foyles bookstore for her first signing, wearing a "Vespa" patchwork dress by Paper London, then headed off to Daunt Books in Chelsea, finding time for a dress and hair change on the way. She arrived in a purple Roksanda Ilincic "Ayden" dress in wool-crepe, with her hair styled in a half-up, half-down do, very reminiscent of the Duchess of Cambridge. Minutes later, Pippa had changed into a black and green dress by hip fashion designer Markus Lupfer to throw a children's Halloween party. Afterwards, she dashed off for her final costume change, reappearing at her evening event in the pièce de résistance: a tweed and black Stella McCartney dress. An exhausting but highly stylish day created a complete shopping frenzy as Pippa fans tried to buy at least one of her gorgeous frocks the following day.

Then when Pippa married James Matthews in May 2017, wearing a stunning Giles Deacon ivory lace bridal gown, she moved effortlessly from the world's most famous bridesmaid to centre stage in the style stakes. Indeed, with the freedom to wear edgier outfits than her royal sister and a fabulously wealthy husband, many observers predict her sartorial sense will continue to develop and she may even land a role of her own in the fashion industry.

OPPOSITE: Jeans and blazers in the King's Road. Kate and Pippa Middleton go shopping in July 2007.

BELOW: Mother-and-daugher style: Kate Middleton and her mother Carole visit the "Spirit of Christmas Shopping" festival at London's Olympia exhibition hall in 2005. Kate's classic Chanel-style tweed blazer smartens up her faded blue jeans.

Carole: the Ultimate Yummy Mummy

With two famously fashionable daughters, mum Carole was never going to escape intense style scrutiny but, thankfully for Mrs Middleton, in her role as family matriarch she cuts an effortlessly elegant figure at every occasion. In fact, with her careful choice of well-cut beautiful garments, Carole has quickly become a flag-bearer for chic, age-appropriate attire, making it crystal-clear where Kate and Pippa inherited their taste and knack for show-stopping outfits.

Like her daughters, Carole chose wisely for the Royal Wedding, sporting a pale blue, wool-crepe coat-dress by Catherine Walker that was a triumph of understated charm. Anxious not to take the spotlight away from her eldest daughter, mum managed to look modern without appearing to try too hard, while still conforming to the conventions of old-school British formal occasion dressing. It came as no surprise, then, that both the Walker ensemble and the equally well-received Gérard Darel suit she wore the following day sold out immediately.

Carole does, in fact, have some experience in the world of

fashion retail, which may provide a little insight into her style savvy. As well as setting up her own successful party supplies mail-order company, Party Pieces, she has used her creative flair to help design the website for high-street clothes chain Jigsaw's "Junior" range. Nevertheless, having the aplomb to dress your age, smartly, is an impressive feat and one that Carole has pulled off time and again. Most recently, she again chose favourite royal designer Catherine Walker to create the blush pink button-down coat-dress she wore for youngest daughter Pippa's 2017 summer wedding. She teamed it with rose pumps, a matching suede handbag and a wide-brimmed hat – looking agelessly chic in the process.

Her beauty and sense of style have not gone unnoticed by those in the fashion world, with designer Karl Lagerfeld commenting: "I think Carole is very sexy. There is something full of life about her. For a woman who must be 50 or so, I think she's great. Full of energy."

Carole has even followed in the footsteps of both her daughters by inspiring a collection of supermarket clothing based on her wardrobe for George at Asda. Brand director Fiona Lambert explained her appeal thus: "Carole Middleton is someone who always really gets it right for her age. She's elegant and stylish, but with a fashion-forward edge."

Kate the Great

Like her fashion-forward mum and style-conscious younger sibling, and even without her royal title, Catherine Elizabeth Middleton would no doubt have grown into an excellent shopper and a stylish dresser. She may even have become a minor trendsetter working within the fashion industry. But it is Kate's fate to, one day, become Queen, a singular destiny that sets her apart from those in the fashion world, including her own mother and sister. And yet if all the expectation and attention are a burden, the Duchess wears it as she does every other item in her wardrobe – with an elegant ease and a supreme confidence. As she is certain to continue evolving as a style icon for many years to come, we can only remark how lucky we are to have Kate as our current and future Queen of Style.

RIGHT: Kate and her family attend the Sovereign's Parade on December 15, 2006, at the Royal Military Academy in Sandhurst.

Kate's Calendar of Style

LEFT TO RIGHT: The young couple at the University of St Andrews, June 2005; Kate modelling the Charlotte Todd transparent dress at the St Andrews Fashion Show, March 2002; Graduation Day, June 2005; Cycling to the gym, July 2005; Participating in the Sisterhood rowing team, August 2007; At the Mahiki nightclub, February 2007; Skiing in Klosters, Switzerland, March 2008.

LEFT TO RIGHT: Channelling sexy 70s style at the Day-Glo Midnight Roller Disco Charity, September 2008; Attending the Diamond Jubilee Tour, Solomon Islands, September 2012; Elegant at Wimbledon in July 2012; Cheering on at the Olympics in August 2012.

OVERLEAF: Unforgettable bridal attire, both by Sarah Burton for Alexander McQueen, the Royal Wedding, April 29, 2011.

The Look Book

The style evolution of Kate Middleton into a modern royal role model has gripped fashion fans the world over. Indeed, in its February 2013 issue, to celebrate Kate's 31st birthday, *Vogue* magazine, the ultimate style bible, undertook an encyclopedic-like look at her dress sense, named Katepedia, an honour bestowed by the magazine only once before – on her grandmother-in-law, the Queen.

Among other things, *Vogue*'s number-crunching discovered that blue is by far Kate's preferred fashion colour, with the Duchess wearing it 24 per cent of the time for official occasions, while a clutch bag is her go-to accessory, with Kate carrying it to over 90 per cent of engagements. The fashion bible also noted that Kate opted for an outfit with a boatneck a little over 40 per cent of the time.

In a similar spirit of admiration and with equally careful attention to detail, we take a forensic look at Kate's most seminal outfits, examining the key looks that helped create a global style queen. From the chic navy lace and nude silk Erdem dress she wore as part of the royal couple's official tour of Canada and North America to the stunning Alice Temperley black lace evening gown she has recycled on two occasions, the Duchess of Cambridge's sartorial selections have sent both lower-end brands and designer sales soaring as fans try to emulate her impeccable ladylike style.

Whether dressed down in an L.K. Bennett sheepskin coat, jeans and Le Chameau wellies to watch Prince William play in a football match, or wowing the crowds in a formal Alexander McQueen scarlet suit during the Queen's Diamond Jubilee pageant, Kate's clothing choices are consistently classic, well considered and elegant.

On nearly every occasion, Kate's outfits reward closer examination. Indeed, the close inspection we offer here merely mirrors Kate's own attention to detail. On official tours of both Canada and the South Pacific and Far East, she has carefully sought out local designers to give a stylish nod to her host, such as when she wore a striking purple and cream floral silk dress by Singaporean-born designer Prabal Gurung to attend a state dinner in Singapore. On other occasions, Kate has even displayed a cute sense of humour, making insider jokes only fashionistas would catch, such as the shoes named after a type of daffodil, the Welsh national flower, which she wore on the Welsh national holiday, St David's Day.

It is both this classic, affordable chic and the subtle personal touches that make a journey through Kate's key looks so inspirational and rewarding. Read on to discover how a pretty girl called Kate, without so much as a stylist to guide her, became a Duchess that dazzled the world.

Shopping Spree Chic

The Dress When Kate decided to do a spot of last-minute honeymoon shopping on April 20, 2011 – just nine days before her wedding to Prince William – she knew the eyes of the world's press would be upon her. So she chose a fittingly restrained yet stylish black wrap-dress for her trip to King's Road, Chelsea – a street that has been synonymous with fashion since its heyday in the Swinging Sixties.

The bride-to-be turned to one of her most trusted labels, Issa, for this key shopping expedition, choosing a smart/casual design with short sleeves, a deep V-neckline and gathered detail at the waist and shoulders. The 100 per cent silk frock hit all the right style notes and ensured she looked sexy yet demure as she strode between stores. And in defying the old adage that royals should only wear black if someone has died, she also demonstrated how she has quietly put her own stamp on Britain's most formal family when it comes to outfit etiquette.

As for Kate's trip – it ended up turning into quite a spree, with the bride-to-be buying several items from UK high-street stores Warehouse and Whistles, as well as US-owned Banana Republic, which she is said to love, as they offer exactly the kind of sleek, fuss-free wardrobe staples she wears so well.

The Shoes Kate teamed her outfit with a familiar pair of tan kitten-heeled, pointed-toed shoes with a gold buckle that she has worn many times before. These particular favourites are designed by Italian label Salvatore Ferragamo, whose unique style of handmade leather shoes are coveted the world over. Founder Ferragamo died in 1960 but during his heyday the Naples-born shoemaker famously worked with many style icons, including Eva Peron and Marilyn Monroe, and his label remains the go-to brand for stylish celebrities from Kate Moss to Carey Mulligan.

The Bag Kate teamed her heels with a Prada bowling bag in a matching shade, with her contrast of tan and black proving once more that she is not afraid to break a few established fashion rules and add a modern edge to classic outfits.

The Jewellery With her wedding just days away, the only jewellery Kate needed to accessorize her outfit was her 18-carat sapphire and diamond engagement ring – a piece that previously belonged to Diana, Princess of Wales. The elegant cluster ring from royal jeweller Garrard sent a clear message so onlookers were left in no doubt exactly which family she was about to marry into!

Stay Unruffled as You Shop

Pounding the high street, racing in and out of different shops to try on a host of new outfits, can leave the coolest fashionista looking distinctly dishevelled. Added to this, Kate knows that even on the most mundane of trips, she is bound to be snapped by a raft of photographers. This has made it doubly important for the Duchess to simplify and refine a workable "day at the shops" look. As always, Kate doesn't disappoint by sticking to a few style-savvy rules ...

Pick a dress with easy access!
Kate's choice of a wrap dress is perfect for clothes shopping. Because it opens at the front, it can be put on and taken off quickly, allowing her to try things on without disturbing her hair and make-up or getting make-up on clothes. This ensures her groomed look is maintained from store to store and that she is not unwittingly snapped looking windswept.

Plump for mid-heels
Kitten heels such as Kate's Ferragamos are an ideal compromise for shopping – they offer more comfort than high heels but are still more glamorous than flats, so she cuts an elegant figure.

Keep hair easy-to-wear
A fiddly up-do is a no-no when trying on clothes, as it will soon be disturbed and end up looking messy by the time you're finished. Kate cleverly opts for a simple blow-dry, finished off with pretty tousled curls, which means a quick shake after each clothing change, and her style looks as good as new.

Choose muted tones of make-up
A shopping session is not the time to try out a new bright lipstick or strong shade of eyeshadow. Chances are you'll end up with nasty smears as you try on prospective purchases. Here, Kate keeps it simple with her trademark barely-there make-up consisting of just enough neutral eyeliner and lip gloss to look fresh and polished. No wonder her preferred make-up brand is Bobbi Brown – famed for its earthy tones and natural finish. Its make-up artist founder, Ms Brown, explains the philosophy behind her products like this: "Women want to look and feel like themselves, only prettier and more confident. The secret to beauty is simple – be who you are."

How to Accessorize like Kate

Kate favours understated jewellery and a minimal colour palette that allows the focus to be firmly centred on her dress and figure. Her sapphire and diamond engagement ring is such a scene-stealer that she ensures all her other pieces complement it rather than compete with it – this navy and nude ensemble perfectly mirrors her sapphire and gold jewellery.

Choose delicate, matching jewellery

Drop earrings and fine-chain necklaces and bracelets are Kate's usual go-to style, and she's abandoned the chunkier rings and heavy earrings from her single days. First seen on her engagement day, her Elsa Peretti "Cabochon by the Yard" necklace from Tiffany's is a simple 18-carat gold chain with a central lapis lazuli cabochon spaced with two round brilliant diamonds. It is often worn with a matching bracelet with three bezel-set diamonds separated by a chain, from Tiffany's "Diamonds by the Yard" collection. Lapis lazuli cabochon drop earrings, set in yellow gold bezel and hanging from a bezel-set diamond stud (see facing page), complement her engagement ring.

Matching your shoes, hat and bag

The 1950s tradition of matching accessories is a style technique favoured by Kate for keeping the whole ensemble tied together. Although indicative of a cautious approach to dressing, keeping to a two-colour schematic, like Kate, does allow the whole look to be sleek, managed and minimal. The essential factor to making this a successful look, however, is adding texture – mixing lace or silk with shiny patent leather, snakeskin or raffia accessories.

LOOK 2

Nude and Navy, Kate's Classic Combination

The Dress Kate wore this stunning navy lace and nude "Cecile" dress for the first day of her Canadian tour in July 2011. During the seven-hour flight, Kate performed a flawless turnaround, changing into the eye-catching dress, which is designed by the hugely fashionable designer Erdem Moralioglu. The scoop-backed, shift dress contrasts stone crepe with a navy lace overlay and flashes a sheer lace sleeve with a scallop detail.

Not only was it a stylish choice, it was a diplomatic one, too. Erdem Moralioglu is based in London but was born in Canada, so it carefully references both nations. The designer is also hot fashion property, with fans including Samantha Cameron, Michelle Obama and Gwyneth Paltrow, helping prove Kate can do high fashion as well as high street. The Duchess's dress is from the designer's Resort 2012 collection.

The Bag Kate sticks to her faithful style of handbag to carry with formal wear: the clutch. This nude animal-print version is from L.K. Bennett, and Kate's been snapped carrying it with many different outfits. And no wonder – its neutral tone means it works well with most outfits.

The Shoes On Kate's feet were her much-loved cream L.K. Bennett "Sledge" shoes that she has worn on several public occasions of late. Predictably, the style soon sold out, both online and in-store, while pairs on eBay were going for nearly double the retail price.

Neutral shoes have definitely become de rigueur recently, with Kate the reigning queen of nude footwear. She relied heavily on the style for her first overseas tour of Canada, and has worn them at many other official engagements, teaming them with a variety of outfits. They are a very flattering choice, as not only do nude shoes elongate the leg, they go with everything, working particularly well as a foil for bold colours or strong prints.

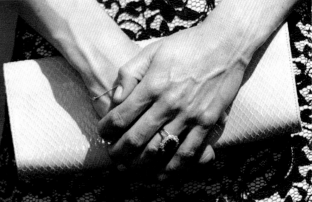

LOOK 3

Kate Recycles with Style

The Dress This white ruffled Reiss dress, chosen here by Kate for a ceremony in Ottawa during her royal tour of Canada in summer 2011, was the same frock she'd worn for her official engagement portrait with Prince William. The "Nanette" dress sold out almost immediately after Kate first wore it and had to be re-issued by the company, with the second lot of inventory disappearing even faster than the original release. The dress features three-quarter sleeves with a cascading frill down the front in a light chiffon fabric. British high-street chain Reiss is a firm favourite of Kate's, and its classic style with a modern twist suits her willowy frame perfectly. It's not the first time the Duchess of Cambridge has worn a garment twice for public events – she makes a habit of rewearing dresses she's worn previously and likes, but usually updates the look with new accessories. The fact that she can successfully recycle old outfits means Kate looks both down-to-earth and confident in her sense of style.

OPPOSITE: This white ruffled Reiss dress Kate is wearing is a perfect example of the popular store's smart but stylish occasion-wear – and demonstrates why Kate so often relies on the brand for formal engagements that others might feel demanded a designer piece. The dress's simple lines are timeless, but the side frill and wrap-over skirt detail echo two key fashion trends of 2011, ensuring it is spot on-trend.

The Hat This scarlet-red felt, beret-style cap with flower embellishments is one of several hats made specifically for Kate's Canadian tour by her favourite milliner, Sylvia Fletcher at Lock & Co. Fletcher is known for creating eye-catching hats and fascinators that are worn by celebrities and royalty alike. The jaunty hat also features Canada's national symbol, the maple leaf, as does her diamond brooch, which was borrowed from the Queen, who lent Kate a selection of pieces from her own personal jewellery collection for the Canadian tour – Kate's first official overseas engagement. By combining her white dress with red accessories, the Duchess is paying homage to the colours of Canada's national flag.

The Bag Kate's gorgeous scarlet and tan woven, fan-shaped clutch – from Anya Hindmarch's Spring/Summer 2011 collection – is a great finishing touch to her outfit and, like the hat, adds a dash of pretty detail and humour to an otherwise simple ensemble. Known for her quirky creations, British fashion accessories designer Hindmarch is a firm celebrity favourite, with fans that include Angelina Jolie, Scarlett Johansson and Sienna Miller.

The Shoes The Duchess is always at her best when mixing high-street with designer accessories, as these vibrant red Albini square-cut court shoes demonstrate perfectly.

Find Your Finishing Touches

After graduating from the University of St Andrews in Scotland, Kate worked as an accessories buyer for Jigsaw, the popular clothes chain that's known for mixing boho chic with classic tailoring. During her time there, she collaborated with the jewellery designer Claudia Bradby, and learned a lot about how to choose those all-important finishing touches. Here are some of her favourite tricks …

Get a good hair buddy
Great hair is a vital part of every well-turned-out ensemble, so it's worth spending time finding a hairdresser who understands your hair and how to get the best from it. Kate entrusts her shiny brunette locks to the Richard Ward Hair Salon just off Sloane Street in Chelsea. As well as performing regular trims, Richard styles Kate's hair for special occasions, which included her wedding.

Plump for pumps
Although she loves a high heel for formal occasions, Kate has worked out that the key to stylish dressing down is neat but classy footwear. Indeed, all of the Middleton women, Kate included, love French Sole – the brand best known for its elegant leather ballet flats.

Polished to Perfection

The Dress Kate dazzled in a regal purple Issa dress as the royal couple attended a concert to mark Canada Day on July 1, 2011. The snug-fitting gown boasted a shallow V-neck and was gathered in the front to accentuate Kate's enviably tiny waist.

Ever since Kate wore a blue Issa London wrap-dress to announce her engagement (see opposite), Brazilian-born Daniella Issa Helayel, the force behind Issa London, has designed a number of bespoke dresses especially for the Duchess. Helayel's designs are instantly recognizable and often feature her distinctive wrap-over shape. Issa dresses are made from a soft fluid silk jersey in a myriad of luminous colours. They often feature figure-flattering ruching and ruffles, creating garments that manage to be the right combination of smart, sexy and comfortable. The Duchess of York's daughters, Princess Beatrice and Princess Eugenie, are also Issa fans.

The Bag Kate carried her black silk "Maud" clutch from the Anya Hindmarch Bespoke collection, which she first showcased when meeting the Obamas earlier that same year. The satiny soft bag is made of 100 per cent silk thread woven to give a super-glossy appearance. Diana, Princess of Wales, also carried the "Maud" clutch, as has Carla Bruni-Sarkozy, Scarlett Johansson and Kate Moss. Anya Hindmarch spoke of how happy she was that Kate chose one of her bags. "It is a real honour and I think she's an amazing pin-up for British fashion," Hindmarch said. "She's a beautiful girl. I love that she's not too 'high-fashion'."

The Brooch Proudly pinned to the Duchess's dress was a diamond, maple-leaf brooch that belonged to Queen Elizabeth, the Queen Mother, and which was given to the late monarch by the people of Canada in 1939. It was passed down to Kate's grandmother-in-law who wore it during her first visit to Canada in 1951. And this tradition was carried on as the Queen loaned it to Kate to wear on her first royal tour of the country in 2011.

The Shoes With her bright jewel-toned dress and eye-catching brooch, Kate kept the shoes simple, slipping into her trusted black Prada heels.

Perfect the Kate Up-do

Kate's go-to hairstyle is long glossy looks, loosely flowing around her shoulders. However, when she wants to make a hair statement, she often sweeps it back into a sleek chignon for a more polished look. Here's how to tame long locks into a chic chignon ...

Separate hair into three sections
The first being midway to the ear, the second up to the crown of the head, and the third being the remaining strands at the back of your head.

Secure the bottom section into a ponytail
Tease the pony to create volume, then wrap it into a bun and secure it with hairgrips.

Split the second section of your hair (at the crown) into two with a diagonal parting
Wrap these two pieces around the bun, with each going in an opposite direction.

Twist the front section of your hair
Wrap it around the chignon before pinning to secure. Finally, spritz with a strong-hold hairspray to keep your "do" in place.

LOOK 5

Kate's Understated Elegance

The Dress While attending a tree-planting ceremony during her Canadian tour, Kate wore this simple but oh-so-stylish metallic grey, short-sleeved, collared shift dress by one of Princess Diana's favourite designers, Catherine Walker. Some fashion critics slammed Kate's choice on this occasion as boring, but to do so is to miss the point of this timeless classic, which looks effortlessly elegant and perfectly accentuates her tiny waist.

The "Kensington" dress was also a very meaningful choice for Kate, as she has multiple family ties to the designer, who died last year after battling cancer. Princess Diana was an enormous fan of Ms Walker's creations, and Kate's mother, Carole Middleton, wore a Catherine Walker ensemble for Kate and William's wedding in April 2011.

The Bag Kate loves a simple but elegant clutch bag, and not only does it look stylish, it's also perfect for giving her something to do with her hands when she's photographed. Plus, clutches have the benefit of not pulling on the shoulders and ruining the line of an outfit, as ordinary shoulder-strap handbags often can. This silver-grey "Somerton" clutch is from Hobbs, another of her favourite high-street chains, especially when it comes to their soft leather bags and shoes. Kate's teamed the look with a simple Links of London silver bracelet with ball detail, which shows off her slim wrists.

The Shoes These rather funky metallic snakeskin "Dela" pumps add a daring touch to an outfit that looks rather staid at first glance. The shoes are by breakout English-born designer Tabitha Simmons and are from her Autumn/Winter 2011 collection. Ever since the Duchess was spotted in her creations, there has been a surge of interest in the model-turned-designer, who unveiled her super-slick debut shoe collection in 2009. Displaying Simmons's signature directional style, every pair of her shoes is handmade in Italy using the finest leather, and features intricate detailing and hidden platforms for extra height. The snakeskin adds interest and daring to an otherwise clean-cut look.

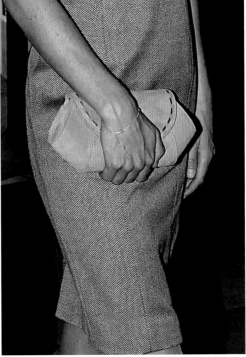

LOOK 6

Nautical Chic

The Dress Kate and William visited Charlottetown, the capital city of the Canadian province of Prince Edward Island (or "PEI", as it is known locally) on July 4, 2011. At a reception to welcome them to the island, she chatted excitedly about her childhood passion for the book *Anne of Green Gables*, which is set on PEI in 1878. The Duchess first read the classic novel by Canadian author Lucy Maud Montgomery when she was eight and she felt an affinity for the title character, Anne Shirley. Her love for the tale may have inspired her choice of dress that morning – as in the movie and television serialization, the character of Anne often sported sailor-collar blouses and full skirts, similar in appearance to Kate's nautical-style, cream cable-knit sweater dress with navy piping around the cuffs and hem, and a silk collar with an anchor printed on it. The £1,100 ($1,780) long-sleeved dress was designed by none other than Sarah Burton for Alexander McQueen, the mastermind behind Kate's wedding dress. In wearing it, the Duchess proved she has an eye for timeless style and that she won't just blindly follow the latest fashion, as this piece was from the designer's 2006 collection.

OPPOSITE: Sarah Burton for Alexander McQueen has dressed Kate for no fewer than eight formal occasions, including in this sailor dress. Since taking the helm as creative director at McQueen following Alexander's death in 2010, Manchester-born Burton has impressively built on the label's considerable success. As a result, she was named Designer of the Year at the British Fashion Awards in November 2011, and included in *Time* magazine's annual list of the 100 most influential people in the world.

Revamp an Outfit You've Worn Before

As a true clothes lover, Kate likes to get good wear out of her favourite pieces. The Queen of Fashion Recycling knows how to prevent an often-worn outfit from looking tired. A year to the day after stepping out in this nautical dress and navy heels in Canada, Kate sported the very same outfit on a trip to Wimbledon's Royal Box. Here's how she kept it fresh …

Keep the setting in mind
The first time Kate wore this McQueen dress, she played up its nautical theme to pick up on PEI's fishing industry. However, the second time around it was the piece's similarity to Wimbledon tennis kits from the 1920s that she was referencing in her sartorial choice. Kate shrewdly realized that the two different settings would bring out two different stories from the same dress.

A change of hairstyle makes all the difference
At Wimbledon, Kate wore the dress with her hair cascading casually over her shoulders, rather than tied back in a loose ponytail, as she did at the more formal event the year before.

Be clever with accessories
The first time she wore the McQueen piece, Kate kept accessories to a minimum so all attention was focused on her dress. But at Wimbledon she paired it with a navy quilted Jaeger clutch, making an interesting fashion statement with the contrasting textures of bag and dress.

The Shoes Kate teamed her dress with simple blue suede courts from high-street store L.K. Bennett, another of her favourite British brands. Its proprietor, Linda Kristin Bennett, was awarded an OBE for Services to the Fashion Industry in the 2006 New Year Honours list. Ms Bennett is renowned for creating shoes that are both practical and glamorous. "When I set out, I wanted to produce something in-between the designer footwear you find in Bond Street and those on the high street," she explains. This makes her designs perfect for Kate, who is the Queen of Practical Glamour.

The Earrings Those diamond and sapphire cluster earrings were a gift from Prince William. They originally belonged to his late mother, Diana, Princess of Wales, and match Kate's engagement ring, which also once belonged to Diana. The earrings are thought to have been a wedding gift from the Crown Prince of Saudi Arabia, and Diana was spotted wearing them at dozens of events during the 1980s and 1990s. Kate put her own personal slant on the earrings and brought them into the twenty-first century by having the studs remodelled into drop earrings.

ABOVE LEFT AND RIGHT: The nautical look is a recurrent fashion theme for Kate, seen above left in a navy double-breasted Alexander McQueen military coat, worn in June 2011, and, above right, in a pencil skirt and blouse by McQueen, this time with sailor-inspired brass buttons, worn in August 2011.

LOOK 7

How Kate Wears Denim

The Jeans Kate certainly loves her J Brand 811 "Olympia" straight-leg jeans, wearing them three times in as many days on her summer 2011 Canadian tour with Prince William. She's also been seen sporting them on numerous other daytime occasions, and here is why: J Brand aren't just any jeans. Kate's discovered that their cut is pretty much the most flattering shape around. No wonder the slim-fitting navy denims have become one of the fashion pack's must-have labels, with fans including Jessica Alba, Nicole Scherzinger and Katie Holmes.

The Duchess no doubt loves that these jeans are free from fuss and obvious branding, but also for the fact that the luxe twill fabric is the perfect shade of inky navy blue and has just the right amount of stretch to flatter her shape.

US company J Brand was founded in 2004 and has soared in popularity over the past few years, thanks to their trend-led styles, such as the "Houlihan" cargo pants and "Love Story" flares.

The Belt This gorgeous butter-soft, chocolate-brown leather belt with brass buckle is by Linda Camm – an accessory designer who has become something of a cult buy and who has enjoyed a huge surge in sales since Kate wore her pieces in Canada. Camm's company is located in Tanzania, where she works with more than 200 Masai tribeswomen to create leather products with exquisite beadwork.

OPPOSITE: The J Brand jeans may have been the talking point when Kate wore this outfit to stroll around Slave Lake in Canada with Prince William in July 2011, but she also chose the occasion to debut what would become another favorite item – her Sloaney One-Button Blazer from the Canadian label Smythe. She has since worn this very versatile piece on numerous occasions, including several times during the London 2012 Olympic Games.

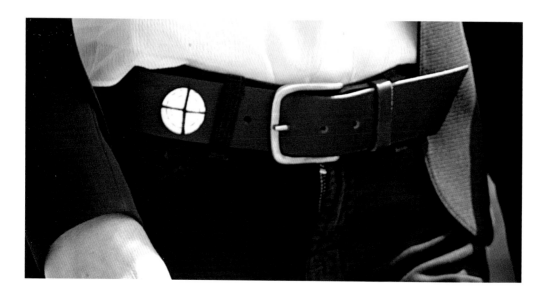

The Shoes Kate shows just how versatile her J Brand jeans are by dressing them up with a pair of black and woven straw L.K. Bennett "Maddox" wedges and navy Smythe blazer, and, later on the same day, working a more casual look with some suede taupe and white Sebago "Bala" deck shoes – traditional boat shoes made in New England, USA. Needless to say, after Kate wore them, the shoes, previously popular only in sailing circles, became hugely popular and sold out in the shade worn by the Duchess.

How to Make Blue Jeans Look Chic

As a true fashionista, Kate knows that you don't need a flashy, high-maintenance outfit to look stylish – a well-fitting, on-trend pair of jeans can see you through most day-to-day situations. Here are a few tips on getting it right …

Pick the right shade
Kate's dark navy J Brands are the ultimate in versatile denim and can switch from casual to super-smart with just a change of accessories.

Make sure your jeans fit
Kate's jeans are the perfect length and size for her frame. Poor-fitting denim looks cheap, not classy – and a designer name means nothing if your jeans are the wrong size or style for your body.

Go slim-cut, not skinny
Kate's cottoned on to the fact that, unless you're a rock star, super-skinny jeans can be just too darn tight to look elegant, so she opts for a slim or straight-leg cut instead. This makes her already-slim legs look even longer and works equally well with a casual checked shirt and flats or a pretty evening top and heels. Unless you want to look like a country and western singer, don't wear a matching denim jacket – wear a cotton jacket or blazer, like Kate.

Cowgirl Kate

The Shirt When Kate attended the Calgary Stampede, an annual Canadian festival celebrating the Western way of life, on July 8, 2011, she truly got into the spirit of the occasion in choosing this aptly named "Rodeo" shirt by Temperley London. Cut from a gossamer silk and cotton blend, the ivory shirt's sheer panels and delicate lace details soften the masculine silhouette of this Western look. The simple but stylish shirt from the label's Pre-Autumn 2011 collection was just one of many Temperley pieces that Kate chose to wear to accompany Prince William on the royal tour of Canada and North America in 2011. The label is named after its creative director, hip British designer Alice Temperley, and is renowned for its blend of timeless designs, sumptuous fabrics and meticulous detail in feminine pieces that embody modern-day "Cool Britannia".

The Accessories With her broad white Stetson and bold belt buckle, the Duchess of Cambridge looked every bit the Canadian cowgirl as she watched the rodeo. William also sported a matching Stetson made of beaver fur felt with a silk lining. The hats were made by Calgary hatmaker Smithbilt Hats Inc., who have been producing this particular style, which has become an iconic symbol for the city of

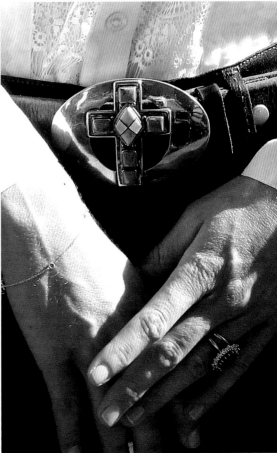

Calgary, since the 1940s. They were presented to the royal couple as a gift after they landed at the Calgary International Airport by the mayor, Naheed Nenshi.

Previous members of the Royal Family to have been given the iconic white hat include Prince Philip, Prince Andrew and Prince Edward. Philip, who received his third hat in 1969, ruffled some feathers when he quipped about not knowing what to do with another hat other than to carry water or plant flowers in it. This prompted the city to give Prince Charles a black cowboy hat when he arrived eight years later.

The Boots While Kate's boots are a traditional cowboy style, like her shirt they are made by a London-based designer. This time she picked the cheekily named R. Soles. The label has sold high-quality boots from its shop on the King's Road, Chelsea, since being established by Douglas Berney in 1975. Kate's boots are the label's "Vegas Setter" style and were designed by Judy Rothchild.

The Jeans No cowgirl outfit would be complete without a pair of boot-cut jeans, and Kate's come from one of her favourite denim labels: Goldsign. The style is named "Passion", and the Duchess plumped for the Habit wash from the label's Autumn/Winter 2011 collection. Cut narrowly on the hip and slender in the thigh, they are made from Goldsign's famously soft, stretchy denim, making them flatteringly form-fitting and comfortable. In other words, perfect for horse riding! According to a spokesperson for Goldsign, sales of their jeans tripled after Kate wore this pair, and the company's web traffic increased tenfold.

Kate is not a fan of obvious branding so it's likely that one of the things she loves about Goldsign, a premium denim line started by Adriano Goldschmied, formerly of AG and Diesel, is its tendency toward subtle brand marks with no distinctive labels or back-pockets to look out for. Kate is said to have bought these jeans from Trilogy Stores in Chelsea, where she has been a regular customer for the last few years.

Embrace Local Style

Wherever she is in the world, Kate never misses out on the opportunity to have fun and experiment with local fashion – and pay a flattering compliment to her host country at the same time. Here's how she cleverly dresses for the occasion while also bringing her own undeniable personal style to play …

Go for authenticity
Kate's hat is from a reputable Calgary hatmaker, not from a tourist shop, and this prevents it from becoming a parody. For true local style, do a bit of research into an area's designers before you travel.

Keep a sense of identity
Kate cleverly mixes pieces from Calgary with Western-style pieces from London-based designers to create a fusion look that effortlessly brings together her British roots and the Calgary culture.

Understand the importance of timing
Eyebrows were raised when William and Kate didn't immediately don their hats at the airport, but by bringing the hat out at the Calgary Stampede, Kate showed she truly appreciated the value of the gift and that she understood the sense of occasion.

The devil's in the details
Kate put thought into every aspect of her outfit, from the cut of her jeans to the size of her belt buckle. Doing so, rather than just adding tokens of local culture to whatever you're already wearing, will make your outfit work as a considered "look" rather than looking like fancy dress.

LOOK 9

Kate's Flight of Fancy

The Dress When Kate stepped off the plane at LAX Airport on July 8, 2011, she was a breath of fresh air in a dove-grey Peridot dress by London-based designer Roksanda Ilincic. The wool-crepe garment is typical of the fluid, draped designs that have made Ilincic a favourite of other high-profile women, including Michelle Obama and Gwyneth Paltrow. With its cap sleeves and pleats that fall from the draped neck to the nipped-in waistband, this piece is ultimately both feminine and flattering.

According to Ilincic, after Kate wore the dress, dozens of customers called her London showroom looking for this piece from her Spring 2011 collection, which had already sold out. Ilincic also heard from several stores who were interested in carrying her line. "This is proof she is a perfect ambassador for British fashion, and fashion in general," Ms Ilincic said.

The Bag This "Natalie" clutch by L.K. Bennett is one of Kate's all-time favourite bags, something she has been spotted carrying on many an occasion. Its diminutive size and neutral colouring make it the perfect multi-tasking accessory, a bag that will work seamlessly with almost any outfit, including something as delicate as the dove-grey dress.

The Earrings Kate's "Grace" earrings are from Chelsea designer Kiki McDonough. Simple yet striking, these £695 ($1,120) white topaz stud earrings framed with diamonds are understated yet still distinctive, which is exactly how Kate likes her jewellery.

McDonough also made jewels for Diana, Princess of Wales. "I once counted Princess Diana as one of my loyal customers and we always had such fun choosing designs for her to wear," McDonough said. "It's a very special added extra that Catherine now enjoys wearing my designs too. As a 'modern Royal', Catherine is as chic when dressed down as she is at formal engagements – my jewellery is designed to be worn every day, and Catherine does this beautifully."

BELOW: Since Kate started patronizing their clutch bags and shoes, British brand L.K. Bennett has become famous around the world for its simple but elegant bags, such as the "Natalie" pictured below. Originally founded in London in 1990 and offering sophisticated shoes and accessories, the store now has outlets around the world and has branched out to produce a range of elegant clothing aimed at meeting the lifestyle needs of modern women like their most famous customer: Catherine, Duchess of Cambridge.

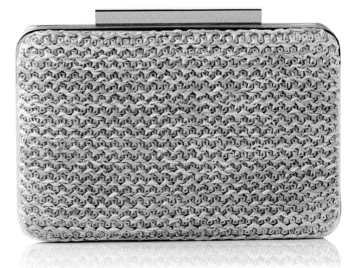

The Shoes Kate's powder-pink "Lovely" stilettos, with a semi-rounded toe and 10.9 cm (4.3 in) heel, are from the Jimmy Choo Spring/Summer 2011 collection. They form part of the label's 24:7 capsule collection of bestsellers and classic styles every woman should own.

Kate recently met the label's founder Jimmy Choo during a trip to Malaysia. Choo, who no longer has formal links with the company he created and then sold, worked with Diana, Princess of Wales, for seven years and thought Kate reminiscent of his former friend. "She is an absolutely beautiful person both inside and out," he said of the Duchess. "Very much like Prince's William's mother. They are both elegant and wear fashion well but, most importantly, are very caring people inside, which is why they appear so beautiful in public."

Look Fabulous after a Flight

As part of her royal duties, Kate has notched up plenty of air miles and it is not uncommon for her to have to meet foreign dignitaries straight off a long-haul flight. It is vital that she looks her best on these occasions but clever Kate has got fresh-faced fabulousness after a flight down to a fine art …

Change out of flight-worn clothes
Sitting in a plane seat for hours will turn most fabrics into an unattractive bundle of creases. But if you make like Kate and have a second pressed outfit hanging in your hand luggage, ready to change into just before landing, you can ensure your outfit will look flawless as you disembark.

Prepare for temperature changes
Kate boarded the plane bound for chilly Canada in a scarlet satin and wool coat-dress by Catherine Walker, perfect for keeping warm, but she knew she'd be emerging under sunny skies in Los Angeles, so she picked out a lighter dress for landing with this in mind.

Moisturize mid-flight
The air on planes is notorious for drying out your skin. For a dewy-fresh glow like Kate's, drink plenty of water and apply moisturizer to your face mid-flight. There's no need to splash out on expensive formulas. Kate has been spotted stocking up on tubs of Nivea Visage Pure & Natural Moisturising Day Cream at Boots on the King's Road.

Prepare your hair
Kate boarded the plane with her hair loosely pinned back, ensuring that it would look fresh and bouncy when she unpinned it, just before disembarking at LAX airport.

Feminine Florals

The Dress On July 9, 2011, the royal couple attended a charity polo match at the exclusive Santa Barbara Polo & Racquet Club, which raised money for The American Friends of the Foundation of Prince William and Prince Harry. For the occasion, Kate turned to one of her favourite failsafe designers: Jenny Packham. The Duchess has worn many a Packham creation over the past few years, as the designer's romantic, feminine style presents a perfect match for the signature look Kate has carefully created. This hand-painted Chinoiserie silk dress in muted blue, sage and peach tones, featuring cap sleeves and piping, gathers at the shoulder and cinches at the waist to flatter the Duchess's willowy frame.

The exquisite fabric is by artists at Chelsea-based interior design firm de Gournay, which specializes in hand-painted wallpapers, fabrics and porcelain in eighteenth-century Chinoiserie (the French term for Chinese style) and nineteenth-century French designs. Packham is a big fan of the design house's prints, and her London boutique features the graphical "Windswept Blossom" wallpaper from de Gournay's delightful Eclectic collection.

The Shoes Kate also showcased a new pair of L.K. Bennett shoes – the patent "Sandy" sandal, part of the company's Signature collection. Thick, smooth straps softly wrap around the foot in a very natural way, making the Duchess's legs appear even longer and slimmer.

The Bracelet On her right wrist, Kate wore her gold "C" charm bracelet, a wedding present from her stepmother-in-law, Camilla Parker Bowles, who owns a similar piece. The disc charm has Catherine's official monogram on one side and Camilla's is on the other. Both Cs are under a coronet, but Kate's C has an extra curl, while Camilla's is surrounded by a circle. For Kate, the bracelet clearly holds strong sentimental value, as it is one that she wears often, and she also owns a silver version of it.

The Bag and the Earrings Kate again carried her boxy L.K. Bennett "Natalie" Clutch, and wore Kiki McDonough earrings – this time, a £495 ($800) pair of beautiful 18-carat yellow gold citrine drops.

Wear Florals without Looking Frumpy

Bold floral prints can be tricky to carry off, but Kate manages to go floral without looking fussy or frumpy. By sticking to some basic style rules, you can do the same …

Keep accessories simple
All-over florals look stunning when paired with sleek sandals and plain accessories, as Kate has done. The smooth, boxy lines of her bag and shoes make for a calming, elegant contrast to the detailed pattern on her dress – anything too fancy would fight for attention with the print and make the outfit look too busy.

Choose a colour
Pick out one feature colour from the floral print to echo in your accessories. Kate has chosen the peachy tones of the dress in her neutral shoes and bag, and in doing so has created a look that is cohesive and polished.

Consider the placement of the pattern
Printed fabrics draw the eye, so look closely at which part of the figure is being highlighted by the placement of the print on the body. The positioning of the flowers on Kate's dress works perfectly with its nipped-in waist, creating an hourglass silhouette.

Jenny Packham

A British fashion designer known primarily for her bridal gowns and lingerie-inspired ready-to-wear collections, Jenny Packham has a way of communicating beauty and allure diffused through French lace and beaded tulle. After graduating with a first-class honours degree from Central Saint Martins College of Art and Design in London, she founded Jenny Packham London – designing eveningwear – and launched her first collection at the London Designer Show in 1988. She has been named as Hollywood Style Designer of the Year, International Couture Bridal Designer of the Year 2007 and British Bridal Dress Designer of the Year 2008 and 2011, and her clients include Keira Knightley, Beyoncé, Cameron Diaz and Jennifer Aniston. The designer's work has been selected for stylistically acclaimed and Oscar-nominated film and television productions, including *Sex and the City*, *The Devil Wears Prada*, *Casino Royale* and *Die Another Day*.

RIGHT: For her June 10, 2011, outing to the Gala for ARK, the Absolute Return for Kids, the Duchess of Cambridge wore a pearlescent rose sequinned gown, embellished with Swarovski crystals, from Jenny Packham's Spring/Summer 2011 collection. Kate paired the dress with L.K. Bennett shoes, staying true to her support of the British high street.

RIGHT: Wearing a silver Grecian-style gown by designer Jenny Packham, draped over one shoulder and gently gathered in at the waist and featuring a bright red poppy, Kate dazzled as she and Prince William entertained 120 guests in the Picture Gallery at St James's Palace on November 10, 2011, at a reception in aid of the National Memorial Arboretum Appeal.

LOOK 11

Kate Does Timeless Glamour

The Dress Even when surrounded by Hollywood's elite, Kate's fashion choices ensure she stands out from the crowd for all the right reasons. Rather than going for a bold colour or a daring neckline or hemline, she cleverly stole the spotlight at a July 2011 BAFTA dinner in LA by covering up in a demure, pastel gown. Small touches, such as the shimmering silver belt and full skirt, gave this somewhat conservative outfit the required amount of drama for the high-profile, formal event.

The glamorous Grecian-style pleated dress by Sarah Burton for Alexander McQueen had a soft scoop neck and was pulled tight at the waist by the belt before unfurling a floaty floor-length skirt. Like Kate's wedding dress, the piece appeared to have been custom made for the Duchess by Sarah Burton. This truly was an iconic look for the Princess, and a replica of the gown currently adorns Kate's waxwork at Madame Tussauds in London.

The Bag Kate stuck with her trusty envelope-style clutch bag, but upped the glamour stakes in opting for this dazzling Jimmy Choo "Ubai" clutch in champagne glitter.

The Shoes For her footwear, Kate also went one step beyond her usual nude sandal staples, stepping out in the aptly named "Vamp" sandals by Jimmy Choo. These glittery silver shoes have an open round toe, crossover straps at the front and a gold buckle-fastening ankle strap. The platform, combined with stiletto heel, makes these dramatic shoes much higher than the classic courts Kate normally wears.

The Jewellery Kate also wore more jewellery than usual for this black-tie gala. On her wrist was a diamond bracelet, boasting a floral cluster design – a large diamond surrounded by smaller diamonds, alternating with baguette diamonds. The bracelet matches the baguette diamonds on her diamond chandelier earrings, which were loaned to her by the Queen especially for the occasion.

Dress Up in Demure Glamour

As a member of the Royal Family, Kate has certain standards to adhere to, so you will never see her in anything vulgar or inappropriate. She always manages to navigate the fine line between looking demure and dowdy. Here's how she pulls off dressing conservatively while still looking incredibly glamorous …

Remember, sexy can be subtle
Rather than choosing a plunging neckline or a short skirt, Kate accentuates her feminine figure by cinching in the flowing fabric of the dress at the waist to create a silhouette with curves in all the right places.

Take it up a level
For the BAFTA dinner, the Duchess wore shoes with higher heels than she normally wears. Stepping out of your comfort zone on special occasions will ensure you look like you've made an effort and haven't just turned up in your everyday clothes.

Colour is key
While bold brights will get you instantly noticed, soft but unexpected shades, such as the lilac of Kate's gown, are far more scene-stealing in a subtle way, as they give you a glowing, ethereal air, which is ultimately more memorable.

Bring on the bling
Kate's sparkling shoes and clutch would have looked over-the-top with an equally glittery gown, but if your dress is demure, it gives you licence to go to town with your accessories.

Whiter Shades of Pale

The Dress Kate cut a willowy but perfectly tailored figure in this oatmeal Amanda Wakeley dress on her visit to The Royal Marsden to meet young cancer sufferers in September 2011. For the royal couple, this was a trip imbued with special meaning, as three decades earlier, Diana, Princess of Wales, had toured the hospital in Sutton, Surrey, on her first solo engagement in 1982. Diana later became the cancer hospital's president – a post that Prince William has filled since 2007.

Princess Diana was famously a big fan of Wakeley's creations, which made the British designer a very appropriate choice for Kate and a stylish way to give a respectful nod to the mother-in-law she never had the chance to meet. Kate's knee-length felt dress featured three-quarter length sleeves, seam details and a slash neck, and was purchased from the Amanda Wakeley Store on London's Fulham Road. The designer later tweeted that the Duchess also bought the same dress in both black and gunmetal – something trendsetters often do when they find a shape that is perfect for them, and a sign that by this point Kate had become very confident of exactly what works as part of her signature "look".

The Shoes Here we see Kate return yet again to her all-time favourite shoes – those taupe "Sledge" heels by L.K. Bennett, which are her brand of choice for high-street footwear. The dedicated Duchess has worn these heels for an exhausting list of occasions, including the Epsom Derby, Prince Philip's 90th birthday, Zara Phillips's wedding, on the royal barge during the Queen's Jubilee celebrations, no less than six times during her tour of Canada in 2011 and to numerous engagements on the tour of Asia in 2012. Her repeated wearing of these heels soon had the "Kate Effect" and single-handedly started the popular trend for wearing nude-coloured shoes with dresses. In fact, for much of 2011 and 2012, no self-respecting woman would be seen sporting any other footwear.

Kate's devotion to this particular style and shade has caused fashion critics to speculate on whether she owns a dozen pairs exactly the same, as they never look the slightest bit worn! We should perhaps give L.K. Bennett the credit, and view this as testament to how well made the shoes are; Kate's continued wearing of them certainly suggests they're both comfortable and durable, despite their 10 cm (4 in) heel. Her "Natalie" gold clutch with its woven straw exterior is another L.K. Bennett design.

The Jewellery On this occasion, the Duchess of Cambridge posed a conundrum for the eagle-eyed press: the curious case of the missing jewels. She arrived at the hospital wearing

her sapphire and diamond engagement ring, but it seemed to have vanished by the time she left, two hours later. Of course, there was a simple explanation. Rather than misplacing it, the Duchess simply stowed it in her clutch bag for hygiene reasons, on the advice of hospital staff.

Along with her ring, Kate also wore her much-loved, diamond-studded silver cross pendant and diamond "Grace" earrings, both by designer Kiki McDonough.

Working Winter White

Kate has said that her favourite colour is white, and she certainly picks a great number of white or off-white shades throughout the seasons. Examples of her preferred hue include the ruffled Reiss dress worn for her official engagement photographs, her Alexander McQueen sailor dress and a selection of Temperley blouses worn on the 2011 royal tour. Here's how she makes this tricky shade work to her advantage – even in the coldest months …

Get the shade right
Outside of June to August, Kate knows it's best to steer away from bright true whites and choose slightly warmer off-white shades such as ivory, cream or champagne, as they look less summery and more elegant.

Don't be afraid to flash a little flesh
If the weather is warm enough – as it was on this glorious late September day – and, like Kate, you still have a summer tan, there's nothing wrong with revealing your legs. By wearing longer sleeves, though, she cleverly ensures the dress is still season-appropriate.

Fabric is key
Forget the cottons and linens of summer – as the weather cools, winter whites should be worn in heavier fabrics with more texture. For the hospital visit, Kate chose a dress of seamed felt, but fine-knit wools such as cashmere, light tweeds or mid-weight jersey would have worked equally well.

Nude rules
For a long time, Kate has known that flesh-toned shoe shades blend into the background with any outfit, while simultaneously making legs look slimmer, longer and shapelier. This makes them the perfect accompaniment to autumn or winter white outfits, rather than white shoes, which can look tacky, or black, which may appear too harsh with a pale ensemble.

Amanda Wakeley

A self-taught designer, born in Chester, who worked for Go Silk in New York before launching her own label in 1990, Amanda Wakeley has developed an international reputation for designing stylish, supremely luxurious, womenswear and accessories. Primarily known for her timeless, luxury eveningwear and pared-down classic daywear, which she describes as "simple ideas expressed strongly", she also has successful shoe and fine jewellery collections. Her ready-to-wear and bespoke creations are sold in the UK, USA, Europe and the Middle East, and she has dressed such stars as Scarlett Johansson, Demi Moore, Kate Beckinsale, Charlize Theron, Jada Pinkett Smith, Helen Mirren and Kate Winslet, and created many of the dresses in the 2012 Bond film, *Skyfall*. She has also dressed many members of royal families, including the late Princess of Wales, whom she provided with many of her most feminine suits, including the bottle-green executive suit Princess Diana wore when she resigned from public life in 1993.

OPPOSITE: Kate wore this floor-length, aqua-coloured Amanda Wakeley evening gown, with flowing Grecian-style pleated chiffon, to her first official solo engagement at the In Kind Direct charity reception in October 2011.

RIGHT: Kate chose Wakeley again here, donning this charcoal knee-length frock, accessorized with an Alexander McQueen belt, for a reception at the Imperial War Museum Foundation in April 2012.

It's a Wrap

The Dress When Kate and William visited Centrepoint's Camberwell Foyer on a chilly December 21, 2011, the Duchess once again perfectly judged the mood of the occasion when picking out her outfit. The dressed-down elegance of Kate's olive-green sweater dress was just what was called for when it came to an event that included a healthy cooking session with some of the homeless young people that the Centrepoint charity supports. The dress is by Ralph Lauren Blue Label, the American brand's most mainstream collection, making it once again that perfect midpoint of aspirational and accessible. Kate may have been covered up in long sleeves and a polo neck, but the form-fitting nature of her lambswool and cashmere dress ensured she oozed classic winter glamour.

The Belt Kate's tight-fitting, wide-gauge belt draws the eye to her size 8 waist and, if reports are to be believed, this was exactly the effect that the Duchess wanted to create. After the event, seasoned fashion followers believe Kate wore this figure-hugging outfit to put an end to the endless pregnancy speculation she faced in the months following the Royal Wedding.

The Boots Kate paired her sweater dress with opaque tights and her trusty "Hi and Dry" boots from Aquatalia by Marvin K. She has worked these on many occasions, unsurprising when you consider the classic calf-high boots are not only stylish and flattering but eminently practical. Advertised as no-slip boots, the resistant rubber soles are topped with weatherproof stretch suede, making them a must-have staple for someone who often has to step out in the changeable British weather. The durability is down to Aquatalia's Canadian founder Marvin Krasnow, known simply as "Marvin K". Witnessing the harsh effects of Montreal winters on women's footwear, Krasnow set out to provide the luxury of looking good while standing up to the elements. Little wonder British fan Kate frequently purchases his creations at UK retailer Russell & Bromley, where they are sold exclusively.

ABOVE: When Kate visited Newcastle's Civic Centre in October 2012, she demonstrated her skill for using a stylish wide belt to dress up a simple outfit and create a more figure-flattering shape. This black leather belt with its large gold buckle is the perfect finishing touch to the plum wool coat she wears here.

Glam Up a Sweater Dress

Wool may not be the obvious choice for a sleek outfit, but Kate has mastered the art of transforming a cosy wardrobe basic – the sweater dress – into a classic seasonal staple. By following her lead, you can look effortlessly chic, even when wrapped up warm for winter …

Balance is key

Kate chooses tights, as bare legs would look unbalanced when paired with black boots, long sleeves and a polo neck. In opting for a pair of opaques, she ensures her outfit looks effortless and composed.

Avoid excess bulk

Wearing wool from neck to knee could add unflattering inches, but opting for a clingy fine knit creates a flattering silhouette.

Best foot forward

To instantly transform a sweater dress from daywear to eveningwear, slip on some sleek high heels.

Belt up

If, like Kate, you want to show off your trim frame, draw attention to your middle with a broad-waisted belt. If, however, you're a little less body-confident, you can fake an hourglass shape by wearing your belt slightly lower, across the top of your hips, to create a smooth line and cover up any lumps and bumps.

Wear studs with high necks

Kate keeps it simple with Kiki McDonough's white topaz and diamond earrings (see opposite).

Kate Gets Her Game On

The Jacket Not one to be left at home by the fire, Kate wrapped up warm in this luxurious chocolate-coloured shearling jacket and braved the elements to watch Princes William and Harry play a Christmas Eve football match in 2011. Part of the L.K. Bennett Signature collection, the "Darwin" coat is a truly timeless piece that we're sure the Duchess will be sheltering behind for many winters to come. With its narrow waist and full collar and cuffs, with exposed shearling, this is the ultimate in classic feminine winter tailoring.

The Sweater Underneath her jacket, Kate layered on warmth with a cosy cream turtleneck "Honeycomb Tunic" sweater by Alice Temperley. The lambswool classic is said to be one of Temperley's first designs, and the honeycomb detail on its collar and sleeves has proved to be so popular that it has become a trademark of Temperley's key collections, with the pattern now featuring on everything from capes to dresses.

Winter fashion is all about luxurious fabrics in textures irresistible to the touch, and you can't get much more tactile than Kate's lambswool sweater and shearling jacket combo. The sweater's slouchy cream collar frames the face perfectly, making a feature of her glowing complexion.

The Jeans Kate's jeans are the Straight jeans by Twenty8Twelve, the label founded by sisters Sienna and Savannah Miller. Both have willowy figures similar to the Duchess, which may explain why their designs work so well on her. These dark blue straight-leg jeans are made from flattering stretch denim, making them ideal for casual day-in-the-park chic.

The Boots Not one to put a foot wrong in the fashion stakes, Kate slipped on a pair of green Vierzon wellington boots by Le Chameau for the game. A French brand, Le Chameau were founded in 1927 in rainy Normandy, and have specialized in upmarket country attire ever since. Their boots are handmade from natural rubber with a luxurious leather lining to keep feet dry and warm on the dampest of days. Kate relies on her trusty Vierzons for any occasion involving outdoor pursuits, and the "Duchess Effect" has not gone unnoticed by the brand.

"Having the Princess regularly pictured in Le Chameau is great news for us," confirms Karl Waktare, managing director of LLC Ltd, which imports Le Chameau products into the UK. "We are the brand of choice for true country people, like Kate."

The Hat Kate completes her look with a brown Australian safari-style hat, which she has owned for many years and often wears on country strolls to protect her trademark glossy mane from the elements.

Look like a Good Sport

Kate has been attending William's sporting events since they began dating, back at St Andrews University. Not one to dress up in tacky cheerleading gear, over the years she has developed her own brand of classic supporter chic. Now you can do the same …

Practical can be pretty
Leave the high heels and spray-on dresses to the WAGs! Wellies or trainers and trousers are far more appropriate for cheering from the sidelines and have their own stylish country feel.

Wrap up warm
There is nothing less attractive than being covered in goose bumps, shivering on the sidelines. Opt for chunky, warm layers that will give you the stamina to stay till the end of the game, no matter how chilly it is.

Comfort is key
Kate's soft fabrics and denim are no coincidence. When you know that you are going to stand around for a while, the right choice of fabric makes all the difference between looking at ease or being uncomfortable.

Keep shapes feminine
Kate's jacket narrows at the waist, meaning that, despite the warm layers, she still shows off her fabulous figure.

LOOK 15

Buttoned-up Beauty

The Coat While many of us may be guilty of overlooking the importance of the right coat for any outdoor engagement, Kate puts a lot of thought into her outer layer. For the unveiling of a plaque by HM the Queen at luxury foodstore Fortnum & Mason, to commemorate the regeneration of the Piccadilly area of London, Kate chose a single-breasted, collarless coat. The twin daffodils on the lapel are to celebrate the date: March 1, St David's Day, 2012.

Selected from the Autumn/Winter 2010 collection of M by Missoni, the Italian brand's more affordable diffusion line, the coat has an interesting fringe trim made from blue bouclé – a type of yarn that produces a knotted, rough-textured fabric. Indeed, Italian fashion house Missoni is famous for its colourful knitwear. The family-run brand was launched in 1953 when Tai and Rosita Missoni began producing their signature crochet-knit designs in Varese. Now headed by daughter Angela, Missoni continues to deliver exquisite collections with inimitable Italian flair.

Kate's choice of coat proved once again that she has a real eye for a style bargain – not only is the coat from Missoni's more affordable line, the Duchess actually picked it up for a discount price in an outlet store. An assistant at the Missoni outlet in Bicester Village shopping centre confirmed that Kate bought the coat there. "We were all surprised to see her and it was great to see her wearing it alongside the Queen."

The Shoes Kate's sense of sartorial fun came into play with her choice of ladylike grey suede pumps by Rupert Sanderson. Like every pair of Sanderson shoes, these "Malone" pumps are named after a daffodil, making them a fitting way for Kate to mark St David's Day and highlighting her incredible eye for detail.

Rather than troubling with elaborate embellishment, Rupert Sanderson's design ethos is "less is more" – his focus is on perfecting the line, balance and symmetry of the shoe to flatter and lengthen the leg. With their rounded toe and slender heels, these understated pumps are a chic and timeless choice, typical of Kate.

The Earrings Kate's ears were adorned with her white topaz and white rhodolite "Hope Egg" earrings by Links of London, previously worn during the official engagement photograph, shot by Mario Testino. Hope eggs are an important symbol in Russian culture, representing hope and new life. Once more the "Kate Effect" was felt in full force after the Duchess first wore these simple earrings, with a fight reportedly breaking out in one New York Links of London store over the last pair!

Snare a Designer Bargain

Kate's known as the "thrifty Royal" for good reason. The Duchess has a real eye for a bargain and is savvy enough to know where to find them …

Hit the outlets
Kate bought her M by Missoni coat at discount centre Bicester Village, which consists of 130 outlet boutiques, including highly sought-after designer brands such as Céline, Dior, Alexander McQueen, Prada and Mulberry, all selling past season and end-of-line pieces with discounts of up to 60 per cent. Queen of the Sales Kate said she loved the discount shopping destination in Oxfordshire as "everything is so contained".

Search for second-hand
Kate is also said to often pick up designer pieces from a second-hand store called The Stock Exchange, near her parents' home in the Berkshire village of Bucklebury. It stocks nearly-new designer clothes by Miu Miu, Issa and Gucci, and is very popular with the locals.

Get in the know
Kate's lucky enough to be courted by fashion industry insiders so she'll always know when there's a sample sale going on. But you can also get in on the insider knowledge by signing up to your favourite labels and boutique mailing lists to receive "early bird" notice of any upcoming secret sales.

Olympic Fashion Feats

The Blazer Selecting a comfortable ensemble for a relaxed visit to the Team GB hockey squad at the London 2012 Olympic Park on March 15, 2012, Kate reworked the classic "Sloane" blazer and jeans look of her youth. The Duchess of Cambridge, here acting as an Olympic Ambassador, mixed high fashion with high-street pieces to create her own take on smart casual. Her double-breasted Punto Milano jacket is by Italian design house Pucci.

Beloved by style icons such as Jackie O, brand founder Emilio Pucci's kaleidoscopic prints were an instant hit during the 1950s. Now under the directorship of Norwegian designer Peter Dundas, the iconic label's bold clothing continues to impress. This particular blazer, however, is a pretty classic piece of tailoring, with its bright gold buttons and shoulder pads, but the exacting cut elevates Kate's look from the everyday to sharp styling.

The Scarf In place of her usual glittering necklace, Kate wore an official Team GB supporter's scarf. The red, white and blue scarf was sold at Next.com, and all profits made from its sale were channelled back into the British Olympic and British Paralympic Associations. As an official Ambassador for Team GB, Kate was expected to wear the scarf several times during the Games. Note how she echoes the scarf's Union Jack colour scheme in her navy jacket, white tee and coral jeans – a clever show of solidarity with the British athletes she was meeting.

The Jeans Kate caused a stir when she stepped out in these coral jeans, and not just because of their vibrant colour. Fashion watchers' tongues were set wagging as it wasn't clear if the pair came from one of her favourite denim designers, J Brand, or if they were a budget choice of "Pop Slim Fit" jeans from Kate's high-street staple, Zara. Around the same time, the Duchess was also spied performing her Olympic duties in a pair of bright cobalt-blue jeans and a vivid red blazer, both from Zara, lending weight to the theory that she was buying her denim on the high street.

The effect of Kate wearing this on-trend shade was immediate. Just 24 hours later, George at Asda witnessed an 88 per cent surge in sales of their lookalike pair, soon to be dubbed "tan-ger-jeans". Fiona Lambert, brand director at George at Asda, said: "Wearing bright colours lifts us all, and now we have the royal seal of approval for coloured denim from Kate Middleton, we know this is going to be the hot trend this summer. Kate looks fabulous in her coral skinny jeans, so girls all over the country will be emulating her style and we expect sales to continue to go through the roof."

As well as anticipating the coloured denim trend, Kate also worked another key look of the season, as she rolled up the jeans' legs to make them three-quarter length. It is exactly these little personalized touches that help make Kate a serious trendsetter.

Find Your Perfect Blazer

Blazers are such a wardrobe staple that every woman should own at least one. They can be dressed up or down, as Kate showed when she wore the same Emilio Pucci blazer with a pencil skirt when presenting medals at the Paralympics later in the month. With a bit of royal fashion know-how, anyone can turn an investment classic blazer into an item to carry them through any occasion ...

The perfect fit
One reason why Kate always looks so chic in a blazer is because she goes for styles that fit like a glove. To ensure yours fits properly, do the arm-lift test – you should be able to raise your arms without the jacket restricting your movement, even when fully buttoned. In addition, the shoulder seam should sit squarely on the shoulders. If the seam is off your shoulders, the jacket is too large and will make you look untidy.

Single or double?
Double-breasted jackets such as Kate's look great on slimmer figures, but if you're curvy, the additional row of buttons can make you appear top-heavy, so stick to single breasted shapes.

Colour coordinate
To get the most wear out of your blazer, select one in a neutral colour such as black or navy, which will then work with every colour of the rainbow. This gives you the option of wearing the same blazer for different occasions, yet making it look fresh every single time. Because Kate's jacket is in classic navy, she can experiment with bright jeans or dress it up with a printed skirt.

Keeping Style in the Family

The Dress Kate made her first public speech as a member of the Royal Family at The Treehouse children's hospice in Ipswich on March 19, 2012. In order to gain confidence for the event, she literally slipped into something familiar. The bright blue "Trina" dress from Kate's high-street favourite Reiss was first worn by Carole Middleton, Kate's mother, at Ascot in 2010. Kate has, in fact, styled it in almost exactly the same way – wearing the thick black waist belt that came with the dress and a pair of simple black heels. Reassuring it may have been, but the outfit did attract one or two negative comments from members of the press who felt that it was just a tad too large for Kate and hung loosely off the Duchess's slender frame.

But while the double-breasted coat-dress was arguably a bit busy, with elements including an oversized collar and scoop pockets designed to draw the eye, Kate still pulls off the look by keeping her accessories simple to create a clean overall outline.

It was also good to see the Duchess sticking to one of her standby British brands, which meant she was helping to boost the UK economy at the same time as giving us all a lesson in family recycling. Her speech, it should be noted, was described as "faultless".

The Fundraising Bracelet Kate's left wrist was adorned with a brightly coloured beaded fundraising bracelet from EACH – East Anglia's Children's Hospices. She is a Royal Patron for the charity that support families and cares for children with life-threatening conditions. Interestingly, the bracelet was designed for EACH by Imogen Sheeran, whose son is the well-known British popstar Ed Sheeran.

The Diamond Bracelet On her right wrist, Kate wore her Tiffany "Diamonds by the Yard" bracelet – a sterling-silver piece adorned with round brilliant diamonds to catch the light, which was created for Tiffany by Elsa Peretti. The Italian jewellery designer is famous for creating understated and timeless pieces, and also designed the necklace worn by Kate when the royal engagement was announced.

The Shoes Kate's patent pumps are the "Angel" style by the label Episode, which is known for its elegant accessories and well-cut clothing and is exclusive to House of Fraser department stores. They have a small platform under the toe, which make them a perfectly practical choice when the Duchess needs comfort in order to concentrate on the task at hand.

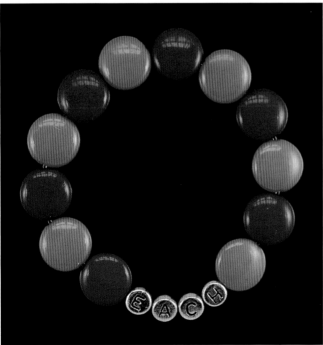

LEFT: Normally a fan of more demure jewellery, Kate raised a few eyebrows when she wore this candy-inspired bracelet, but it quickly transpired that it was in support of a charity close to her heart. The bright purple and orange beads, which featured four round metallic stones that read EACH, was specially commissioned for the East Anglia Children's Hospice. The bracelet's designer, Imogen Sheeran, is mother to singer-songwriter Ed Sheeran, and much of Sheeran's jewellery, including this piece, is said to be inspired by Ed's favourite sweets.

OVERLEAF: Kate shows off her bold colour-blocking sartorial skills with these two strikingly elegant ensembles. The flowing red silk jersey "Sarai" evening gown, left, with billowing sleeves, plunging V-neck and sash waist, is by Beulah London, worn when she and Prince WIlliam attended a gala for the Child Bereavement Charity in October 2011. The canary-yellow Jaeger shirt-dress, right, was worn for her visit to the Solomon Islands in September 2012, and features a full, pleated skirt and tie-waist.

Wow in Primary Colours

Primary colours make a big impact and draw a lot of attention. You have to be confident in your fashion choice to wear a block of bold colour as Kate often does on formal occasions, like the 2012 Jubilee engagements. In making brave fashion choices, she was honouring the importance of key events during a special year for the Royal Family. Here's how you can create the right impact with colour …

Red – Bear the season in mind
There is an important distinction to be made between rich festive red and hot summer red. Brighter shades such as the scarlet Alexander McQueen dress worn by Kate aboard the royal barge during the Thames Diamond Jubilee Pageant evoke the freshness of summer without any of the heaviness of deeper winter tones, such as berry.

Yellow – Dare to turn heads
A bright yellow dress is definitely a defiant fashion choice – it's a shade that simply demands attention. Avoid diluting this affect by wearing yellow with other colours, though. Be brave and make yellow the solo hero of your outfit, just as Kate did when she paired her yellow Jaeger shirt-dress with nude heels when visiting the Solomon Islands on her royal tour in September 2012.

Blue – Be bright
Blue is often seen as a neutral colour, especially in darker shades like navy. But blue can make just as much of a statement as other primaries if you opt for bright shades, such as Kate's electric-blue Reiss dress, seen on page 78.

Kate's Animal Attraction

The Dress April 25, 2012, was a fashion first for Kate when she wore celebrated British designer Matthew Williamson on a visit to the British Film Institute for the London première of *African Cats*. The royal couple were there to see the Disney documentary, which had been made in conjunction with the Tusk Trust – a charity Prince William has been a Royal Patron of since 2005. The feature film tells the story of a family of cheetahs and a pride of lions, and aims to raise awareness and funds for the animal protection charity.

Kate had never previously worn anything by designer-to-the-stars Williamson for an official occasion, but his beautifully cut gowns featuring vivacious embroidery and eye-catching detailing fit perfectly into the Duchess's existing fashion repertoire. This sleek grey dress is from Williamson's Pre-Autumn 2012 collection and features ornate beading, an exposed zipper in the back and the subtle peplum detailing that Kate became so fond of in 2012.

The dress has three-quarter length sleeves and deep turquoise and gold beads around the neck and sleeves. Williamson added more beading at the neck especially for Kate's frock, which was not present on the catwalk version. As well as being signature Williamson flourishes, the bead embellishments cleverly harmonized with the film's African vibe.

Matthew Williamson's label is now 15 years old, during which time the graduate of the famous Central Saint Martins College of Art and Design in London has become renowned for celebrity-beloved butterfly print dresses and his line of bridal gowns and accessories. In 2011, the designer also launched a more moderately priced collection – MW Matthew Williamson – and has had a high-street collection – Butterfly by Matthew Williamson – available at Debenhams since 2009. These easily affordable lines have brought a taste of his luxurious and feel-good designs to the masses without compromising the integrity of his core approach – no mean feat for such a high-profile designer!

The Earrings Once more, Kate turned to her favourite jewellery designer, Kiki McDonough, for her stunning blue topaz and diamond pear earrings that perfectly dovetail with the detailing on her dress. The eye-catching "Kiki Classic" earrings soon became runaway bestsellers, despite their rather hefty price tag of £1,200 ($2,000).

The Shoes and Bag Kate let her dress do all the talking by pairing it with these understated carbon-grey suede "Valerie" pumps and matching clutch bag, both from British shoe designer Emmy Scarterfield, a favourite of the Duchess. She also has the same shoe and bag combination in brown. Scarterfield is the founder of the luxury custom-made wedding and dress shoe brand Emmy Shoes. Having worked in Milan, designing shoes for five years, she set up the brand after struggling to find comfortable but pretty occasion shoes.

Perfect Occasion Make-up

Kate always manages to fit her cosmetic choices to perfectly suit the occasion, and with her consistently flawless skin, glowing cheeks and expertly defined eyes, it's hard to believe that most of the time she insists on doing her own make-up! Here are some of her easy-to-follow tricks …

Look after your skin
You only have to look as far as mum, Carole, to see that Kate owes her amazing complexion in part to good genes. But the Duchess is also said to stick to a consistent cleanse, tone and moisturize skincare routine, wherever she is in the world. This means she usually only needs a touch of light foundation or tinted moisturizer as a base.

Keep colours neutral
Kate is never one to shy away from colour, but she saves it all for her vibrant wardrobe, which is full of rich jewel tones. When it comes to make-up, her cheeks tend to have a subtle rosy-pink flush, while on her lips she usually goes for a gloss just a shade or two darker than her natural lip colour.

Pick one feature to emphasize
The beauty rule goes: eyes or lips, but never both. Kate follows this rule religiously and pretty much always plumps for eyes. She rims both her upper and lower lash lines with black eyeliner and a generous layer of mascara. This creates a look that is always striking, but never overdone.

Pale but perfect nails
When you have a stunning wedding band and eye-catching sapphire engagement ring to show off, you don't want to upstage them with brightly coloured nail polish. Kate's nails are always neatly trimmed and filed, and tend to be covered with a simple baby-pink varnish.

The Striking Appeal of Teal

The Dress On May 11, 2012, Kate and Prince William were guests of honour at the Greatest Team Rises Olympic gala event – an official launch party for Team GB and ParalympicsGB, which helped mark the final countdown to the London 2012 Games. For such a high-energy occasion, Kate wowed in one of her bravest fashion choices to date: this stunning Jenny Packham teal ballgown, marking a welcome return to one of her favourite designers. She chose a bespoke version of Packham's "Aspen" gown, which first appeared on the catwalk in a pale green shade as part of her Spring/Summer 2012 collection.

The neckline was also more demure than the catwalk gown, with extra gathered fabric in the bodice and slightly higher lace at the décolletage and shoulders. But Kate's head-turning teal shade drew maximum attention to a design that boasts beautiful silk chiffon, lacy cap sleeves, an ornately embellished bodice, bejewelled waistband and flowing pleated skirt. Perhaps the most show-stopping feature was the gown's button-up back, made entirely from lace and dotted with sparkling Swarovski crystals – beautifully delicate, but also subtly sexy.

Of course, this was far from the first time Kate had turned to Jenny Packham to pack a red carpet punch. The Duchess has worn the British's designer's regal creations on many previous occasions, including the silver one-shoulder gown accented by a velvet ribbon that she wore as host of a charity dinner at St James's Palace in November 2011, and the dazzling pearlescent rose sequin gown, again decorated with Swarovski crystals, worn at the ARK children's charity gala dinner in June 2011, which was the first event attended by Kate and Prince William as a married couple.

The Hair This is one dress that demanded an "up-do" rather than Kate's beloved loose-flowing blow-dried waves, and the Duchess elected for an elaborate style featuring multiple braided sections forming an intricate chignon. An elegant knotted bun, put in place by the team from the Richard Ward salon in Chelsea that Kate – and her family – have long frequented, showed off the elaborate bodice design on the reverse of her dress to full effect. The swept-to-one-side parting – a new look for Kate – also gave the style added height and impact from the front.

The Shoes and Bag Kate accessorized the striking dress with a matching bespoke clutch bag, again by Jenny Packham, made from the same silk as the gown and a layer of the brocade used in its side panels. The look was completed by a pair of high-octane glamour Jimmy Choo platform "Vamp" sandals, in distressed silver leather, which she has worn on other occasions.

The Finishing Touches The Duchess completed her glamorous look with silver teardrop-shaped diamante earrings. Her make-up, meanwhile, featured the new addition of some shimmery eyeshadow to complement her signature smoky black mascara and eyeliner, plus a shiny pale pink gloss for her lips.

Channel 1950s Glamour like Kate

For show-stopping events, Kate often favours a classic 1950s-style lace and silk formal gown. This was first seen in her vintage choice of wedding dress by Sarah Burton for Alexander McQueen, but you can also note the 1950s flavours in this teal Jenny Packham number. It's a look that openly references former Hollywood film icons and was most typified by the effortless chic of another regal style icon: movie star and Princess of Monaco, Grace Kelly. So it's no surprise that similarities were drawn between Kate's choice of wedding gown and the lace-bodiced number worn by Kelly for her marriage to Prince Rainier in 1956. Here's how to borrow some of this retro look ...

Draw attention to your waist

Tiny middles are the order of the day for any fifties' bombshell, and Kate draws attention to her hourglass figure by choosing frocks that gather in tightly at the waist.

Find a fitted bodice

For this look, above-the-waist dresses should be tight fitting and, ideally, have a sweetheart neckline. Gowns tend to be strapless and bare-shouldered, although a thin veil of see-through lace or chiffon is often stretched over the décolletage and arm area for a demure finish.

Full-length flow

Although full, prom style skirts were very popular in the 1950s, not all evening gown designs were dominated by this look. Long, sleek lines were also in vogue, as echoed here in Kate's Jenny Packham frock, and styles were sometimes reminiscent of wedding gowns or nightgowns. To emulate this look, the fabric should be silk or satin, the dress floor-length, fitted at the waist and oozing a mixture of class and old-fashioned sex appeal.

Don't forget to sparkle

Finishing touches are all-important for true movie-style glamour, with Kate and Grace Kelly both favouring diamond or diamante embellishments sewn into gowns and onto clutch bags, and showcasing the same precious stones when it comes to earrings and necklaces. This ensures the maximum light is reflected when those inevitable flashbulbs go off!

LOOK 20

Polo with Polish

The Dress When you're a spectator, it's never a good idea to draw attention away from the main event. So when Kate went to watch Princes William and Harry play polo at the Audi Polo Challenge at Coworth Park in Berkshire in May 2012, she chose a pretty, yet subtle green dress.

The frock in question is the "Rebecca" dress from another label Kate loves to wear: Hampshire-based British designer Libélula. This knee-length dress, from the label's Autumn/Winter 2011 collection, is 100 per cent silk and features side pockets, plus piping at the stand-collar, cuffs and waist.

Kate chose the buttoned-up printed shift in the popular "mermaid blue and brown petal" colourway, but the dress also came in a brighter emerald green with cream petals, a plain green (see right, centre), and a black-and-white dot, as well as a more formal version in black velvet.

It is perhaps no coincidence that the Libélula line is designed by Sophie Cranston, who early in her career worked with two other labels adored by Kate: Alexander McQueen and Temperley. In fact, the Duchess is such a firm fan of Libélula that, ahead of the Royal Wedding, Cranston was heavily tipped to be Kate's dress designer of choice, although Sarah Burton for Alexander McQueen famously won the final commission.

Nevertheless, Cranston's vibrant prints and timeless shapes, crafted from luxurious fabrics, have proved popular with a number of celebrities, including Emma Watson and Jerry Hall. One of the more notable Libélula items that Kate has also worn is the "Dulwich" coat – a black velvet number that sold out hours after she was snapped wearing it to a friend's wedding in January 2011.

The Shoes Kate donned a pair of camel Stuart Weitzman "Minx" espadrilles to match her green dress – towering wedges that made her legs look even longer and more defined than usual. Each shoe base is crafted from cork and boasts a huge 11-cm (4.5-in) heel, so they're not for the faint-hearted. However, despite their vertiginous shape, the espadrilles actually demonstrate Kate's practical side. After watching William play polo for more than 10 years now, she is well aware that wedges are actually a perfect choice since they won't sink into the grass. The wedges are especially useful during the popular ritual when spectators are called upon to "tread in the divots" between chukkas. This amusing but crucial part of polo involves stamping in loose pieces of turf that the ponies have kicked up during the game, helping to ensure the grass is as flat as possible before play is resumed.

Country Chic with a Modern Twist

Whether she's smart in a simple frock or more dressed-down in jeans and boots, Kate knows exactly how to work country style like a true native. It's a look that has its roots in jodhpurs and riding boots, and floral Laura Ashley-style dresses, but this uniform has been updated by the Duchess to include skinny jeans, long leather boots and more stylish designer frocks. This cleverly ensures she fits in seamlessly with the smart country set that she has married into, while maintaining her own signature style. Here are some of the key fashion rules for fitting right in ...

Try some tweed

It doesn't have to be stuffy or boring – in fact, this once old-fashioned fabric has recently made a comeback. Kate knows that, when used in moderation, tweed can look fabulous in the form of a fitted jacket or simple accessory, such as a tote bag.

Wear shoes you can walk in

Kate appreciates that no outdoor event is much fun unless you can move around comfortably all day. The ability to move quickly is especially vital as she so often brings the young couple's much-loved dog, Lupo, with her for this kind of event. Here, she's wearing wedges, but she is just as frequently seen in long, flat-heeled, leather riding-style boots.

Give it some welly

With all the rain in the UK, good wellies are a countryside necessity – and thanks to the popularity of music festival chic over the last 10 years, the humble Wellington boot has been brought to the forefront of fashion. Wellies now come in a rainbow of colours and prints, with designers such as Marc Jacobs and Patrick Cox making their own limited edition pairs featuring edgier details such as bejewelled buckles, high heels and mock-croc textures. Kate used to be seen in popular high-end Hunters, but in 2012 switched to a pair of green Vierzon boots by French brand Le Chameau, sparking press speculation of a "wellie war" between the rival brands!

Libélula

Designed by Sophie Cranston, Libélula is an innovative up-and-coming British design house based in Hampshire.

After starting her career in fashion in the backrooms of Savile Row and Bellville Sassoon, Cranston went on to work for Alexander McQueen himself, and then set up Temperley in 2000 with Alice Temperley. After a move to the south of Spain, Cranston founded Libélula, meaning "dragonfly" in Spanish. A return to the UK saw the brand expand into many of the leading boutiques and also internationally.

Known for its vibrant prints and timeless and flattering shapes, as well as Cranston's innate sense of colour and use of luxurious fabrics, the label creates classics with a twist, like the elegant, black velvet "Dulwich" frock coat with a diamante clasp, seen here. Libélula also has a range of wedding dresses and bridesmaids dresses in their signature shapes and fabrics.

The "Kate Effect" has benefited the company. "Kate has helped the business enormously," Cranston told *Vogue*. "She has had an amazing effect on the label." In describing the inspirations that drive the label, the designer says, "I have tried to make dresses that can be worn every day with some eveningwear ... I have mixed fabrics: such as velvet with lace, and wool with lace, as well as different silks mixed together."

LOOK 21

Pretty in Pink

The Dress Kate chose to wear this dusky pink formal Emilia Wickstead coat-dress for the World Sovereign's lunch to celebrate the Queen's Diamond Jubilee at Windsor Castle on May 18, 2012. The dress needed to feel suitably regal, as the event was attended by an impressive who's who of modern royalty, with over 60 attendees from around the globe, including an impressive 24 kings and queens!

Made from double-wool-crepe, the soft pink frock with a full pleated skirt featured a fitted bodice, with concealed off-centre closure and an inset waistband. The minimalist approach, with long sleeves and modest hemline, made for a fittingly demure effect, considering the esteemed company.

Kate's made-to-measure coat-dress came from Emilia Wickstead's Spring/Summer 2012 collection, featuring a pretty array of candy-box colours, and was described by the designer as being a "mixture of sophistication and playfulness – for fashionable women who entertain".

The Duchess of Cambridge has been one of Wickstead's most famous fans, opting for her garments on numerous public engagements when the eyes of the world have been upon her, and Kate has also been spotted several times visiting the designer's atelier in London's Belgravia.

Kate particularly loves Wickstead's signature smart-but-simple coat-dresses and wore one in March 2012 for a St Patrick's Day parade, when she dressed appropriately in green, and later in July 2012, choosing a pale primrose creation when her husband, Prince William, was awarded the Order of the Thistle.

British-based, New Zealand-born designer Emilia Wickstead has fast become one of the go-to designers for London's high society. Despite only setting up her label in 2009, she has already dressed a number of notable clients, including Kate's cousin Lucy, fellow designer Anya Hindmarch, Lady Kitty Spencer, Emma Parker Bowles and India Hicks, bridesmaid to the late Princess of Wales. But Wickstead's client base is not restricted to the upper echelons of the aristocracy; she can also count popstar Dannii Minogue and the Prime Minister's fashion-forward wife Samantha Cameron as trusted customers, both of whom have worn her chic designs many times.

The Shoes and Bag To set off the coat-dress, Kate recycled a pair of champagne-coloured satin Prada pumps and a Prada clutch bag that we have seen on multiple occasions. These versatile accessories perfectly complemented the frock's pink hue.

Wear Pale Pink – without Fading into the Background!

Pink is never the easiest colour to pull off, but Kate manages it with style and flair. Here's how to wear pale pink to perfection …

Keep skin tones warm
Pastel and dusky pinks can be tricky shades to wear, as their cool tones can easily drain colour from your skin. But canny Kate chose to wear this soft colour in early summer when she had a light tan, and also applied plenty of her signature rosy-pink blusher so her complexion was a picture of glowing health.

Mix shades
Like Kate, try wearing a deeper shade of pink when it comes to your shoes and handbag to offset the paleness of the dress.

Choose sumptuous fabrics
As with white, pale shades of pink look classiest in slightly heavier, more luxurious weights of fabric, so garments don't become transparent and end up looking cheap. Kate chooses wool-crepe here, but cashmere, raw silk and felt would also work well.

Be a grown-up Team pink with frills or fussy styles and you risk looking far too girly. Kate avoids making this fashion faux pas by opting for an elegant, streamlined dress style that oozes restrained glamour.

Regal Recycling Clever Kate again demonstrated her thrifty side by giving a second outing to the pricey £1,200 ($2,000) pink dress at her first Royal Garden Party at Buckingham Palace just two weeks later, to kickstart the Diamond Jubilee celebrations. The Royal Garden Party is a long-held annual tradition hosted by the Royal Family in celebration of those who have made a worthy contribution to public life, and they are invited for tea and cakes in the Palace grounds. It's always a special day, but this year's event was imbued with extra sentiment because it marked the Queen's 60 years on the British throne. In the same month, royal historian Sir Roy Strong claimed that the Queen herself approved of the Duchess's willingness to wear the same outfit twice, rather than always sporting something new. It is certainly something of a royal tradition, with the Queen herself having been spotted revisiting favourite outfits many times during her long reign.

The Hat When wearing the dress for the second time, Kate kept things fresh by accessorizing it with a new pink hat by Jane Corbett. The milliner shared her excitement at seeing Kate wearing her design by taking to her blog: "Absolutely thrilled that HRH The Duchess of Cambridge chose to wear one of my hats to her first Garden Party at Buckingham Palace this afternoon," she gushed. "How wonderful!"

Emilia Wickstead

Born in New Zealand, the designer spent her formative years in Milan before graduating from Central Saint Martins College of Art and Design in London in 2007. While living in New York, Milan and London, Emilia worked in the design studios at Giorgio Armani, Narciso Rodriguez and Proenza Schouler, and at *Vogue*.

She founded Emilia Wickstead in 2008 in London, with showrooms in Chelsea and Knightsbridge, and launched her flagship store in Belgravia in 2009. A ready-to-wear collection is housed in tandem with made-to-measure garments. Noted for their pretty colours, demure style and tiny waists with pleated or A-line skirts that give a feminine, hourglass shape, the clothing is certainly "fit for a princess". Focusing on simple and sweet designs and a modern interpretation of English classics, the designs suit Kate perfectly, such as the yellow coat-dress, right, worn at St Giles Cathedral after the Thistle Ceremony on July 5, 2012, in Edinburgh, and the belted emerald dress worn with a Lock & Co. hat for presenting St Patrick's Day shamrocks to the Irish Guards in Aldershot, Hampshire, on March 2012, far right.

Resplendent in Royal Red

The Dress Kate wowed in this vibrant scarlet Alexander McQueen dress for one of the most spectacular events of the entire Royal Diamond Jubilee celebrations: the Thames Diamond Jubilee River Pageant on June 3, 2012. The regatta saw the largest number of boats ever assembled on the River Thames sailing down the river, including the royal barge – *Spirit of Chartwell* – which was decorated with over 10,000 blooms, and carried HM the Queen, the Duke of Edinburgh, the Prince of Wales, the Duchess of Cornwall, the Duke and Duchess of Cambridge and Prince Harry.

Keen to blend in seamlessly with the most senior members of the Royal Family, Kate knew she couldn't go wrong by choosing her go-to designer for major events, Sarah Burton for Alexander McQueen. The bespoke frock incorporated multiple McQueen design elements, including the fitted dress and pleated skirt, and most resembled a wool-crepe dress from the label's Pre-Autumn 2011 collection. Longer sleeves have been added and the hemline lowered to mark the formality of the occasion, while the standard boat-neck was perhaps a nod to the maritime occasion itself.

Kate has previous form when it comes to this particular shade of red, wearing a "Marianne" coat-dress in the same hue by Catherine Walker on the final day of her tour of Canada in 2011. Unusually for the Duchess, versions of this McQueen dress had also been worn by two high-profile celebrities before her: American reality TV star Kim Kardashian and UK *X Factor* judge and popstar Tulisa Contostavlos. But it is, of course, Kate who was credited for helping British label Alexander McQueen's UK and worldwide sales soar by nearly 30 per cent between 2011 and 2012 – a profit increase that means the label has now overtaken the sales of the previous British frontrunner, Stella McCartney.

The Brooch and Scarf Kate also wore a rather fitting new brooch, in the shape of two silver dolphins. It was a wedding gift from the RN Submarine Service, of which William is Commodore in Chief, and was perfectly in tune with the pageant's maritime theme. Meanwhile, Kate's cashmere scarf boasts the distinctive pattern of Strathearn tartan, and was clearly a respectful nod to the Scottish title she inherited on her marriage: the Countess of Strathearn.

The Bag and Shoes Toning perfectly with the dress, Kate's bag was a modified version of the Alexander McQueen Classic Skull Clutch with Silk Bow, in which the jewel-encrusted skull (perhaps seen as inappropriate for this formal day of celebration!) was replaced with three large bespoke rhinestones. Avoiding the obvious choice of matching shoes, Kate wore her much-favoured L.K. Bennett "Sledge" pumps in nude, a decision much debated by fashion commentators, but it did have the advantage of lengthening her legs and lending the dress a more summery feel.

The Hat Kate's flamboyant scarlet cocktail hat was by Sylvia Fletcher, for royal milliner James Lock & Co, and perfectly fitted the mood of the occasion. Fletcher also designed the Duchess's distinctive red maple-leaf hat worn on her tour of Canada in 2011.

Bringing a Modern Twist to Formal Occasions

Befitting the fact that she is representing a younger, more accessible breed of Royal, Kate has helped shake up formal dress protocol. In choosing edgier designers and fashion-forward accessories, she adds a fresh feel to timeless, classic pieces. Luckily, her modern smart style is easy to replicate without spending a fortune …

Choose skirt shapes with care
Rarely does Kate go shorter than knee-length when it comes to skirts and dresses for formal occasions, but in opting for either a classic A-line shape – or a pleated fuller shape, as at the river regatta – she creates a look that is flattering and feminine, never frumpy.

Belt up
The Duchess loves to use a belt to add shape at the waist of suit jackets and wool dresses. This lends a touch of fashion flair and sex appeal to outfits that can otherwise lack form.

Dare to flare
When Kate wears a knee-length skirt suit or dress, she often pairs it with a more modern short blazer with a slight flare or peplum, bringing the outfit bang up to date.

Shoe savvy
Matching smart outfits with modern high heels, especially with a fashionable wedge shape, means the Duchess stands out from the rest of the Royals, parading their sensible court shoes. Younger women can still identify with Kate's style, too.

Stay ahead of the game
Red, blue, white or black; lacy, feathered or wool … Kate's headwear choices are wide-ranging, and it has been noted by fashion critics that no one wears a hat quite like the Duchess. Her trick is always to judge it just right for the occasion, as with this perfect red Sylvia Fletcher number at the river pageant. To make like Kate, favour the smaller ornate hats or fascinator shapes that won't cast shade over your face, and be bold with striking colour choices – so long as they exactly match the key colour of your outfit.

Kate Epitomizes Understated Elegance

The Dress Sarah Burton of Alexander McQueen has long been Kate's go-to designer for high-profile events, so it was no surprise when the Duchess turned up at St Paul's Cathedral for the Jubilee Service of Thanksgiving on June 4, 2012, in a sensational custom-made dress by Burton.

It was, in fact, the third day in a row that Kate had chosen to wear an Alexander McQueen piece to the weekend of Diamond Jubilee celebrations – and she saved the best for last. The slim-fitting, nude lace shift has a white sheath underlay and satin waist detail. Like all the McQueen gowns that Kate favours, the dress has long sleeves, which when coupled with the knee-length hemline and boat neck, give the outfit a modest, ladylike appearance, despite its form-fitting bodycon shape.

This piece was custom-made for the Duchess by the British label, but that didn't deter copy-Kates from clamouring to re-create the look. Within hours of the Duchess arriving at the 10 a.m. service, supermarket chain Asda reported a 35 per cent rise in sales of a roughly similar nude lace dress retailing at £25 ($40), and by the end of the day, the piece was completely sold out. Never one to miss a Kate-created publicity moment, Asda brand director Fiona Lambert observed, "We expect the Kate phenomenon to continue as she has now established herself as a British style icon. We know our customers can't wait to see what she will be wearing next."

The Hat Kate's delicate beaded cocktail hat, with silk tulle, organza discs, veiling and smoked quartz detail, was created by Jane Taylor, a Fulham-based milliner who trained under former milliner to the Queen, Marie O'Regan. It was the first time that Kate had worn one of Taylor's creations, but it wasn't the first time Taylor had created headwear for the Royal Family. Zara Phillips, Princess Eugenie and Sophie, Countess of Wessex, have all worn her hats to official events before, and the Countess also sported one in St Paul's that day.

"Both the Countess of Wessex and the Duchess of Cambridge look stunning," an understandably jubilant Taylor said at the time. "They both have a unique yet timeless sense of style and wear hats so well! It's a dream to have two members of the Royal Family wearing my pieces to such an important event." The milliner then went on to reveal that Kate's hat took about eight hours to make, and that the Duchess "chose a cocktail hat because it's a happy medium

between a fascinator and a more formal, bigger hat that covers the head".

The Duchess also wore the hat slightly off-centre and apparently spot-on, according to Taylor: "You should always wear hats at a jaunty angle, and Kate positions them at exactly the right angle, which makes them look flattering, and she teams them with classic outfits so they look elegant." Perhaps unsurprisingly, as soon as the Duchess was pictured wearing the hat, Taylor was bombarded with emails and orders from all around the world.

The Bag For the church occasion, Kate stuck to her favourite style of modest handbag – the box clutch – and carried the Prada satin logo bag tucked neatly under her arm.

The Earrings Kate kept fashion commentators guessing about where she picked up her dazzling "diamond" and "pearl" drop earrings. So it came as a shock to many when it was revealed that they were in fact a cubic zirconia pair from independent and affordable jewellery website Heavenly Necklaces.

The company's founder, Belinda Hadden, who designed the earrings, was astonished to learn that Kate had worn her creations to such a high-profile event. It wasn't long before the "Kate Effect" began to take hold. "Within the next 24 hours, I had sold out," said Hadden. "I sold 60 on my website, which is the amount I would usually sell in a whole year. They are made of finest grade cubic zirconia, but what makes them look as authentic is the settings they are in."

The Shoes Kate mixed designer and high-street pieces with her usual flair by anchoring the outfit with her favourite nude L.K. Bennett "Sledge" heels. These handy heels have a small platform that cushions the toes and makes them comfortable to wear all day. At the St Paul's service that day, Samantha Cameron, wife of Prime Minister David Cameron, wore the same pair of shoes – only in black!

Wear Formal Hats with Flair

A formal hat is one of the most transformative pieces you'll ever wear. It instantly adds a sense of occasion and drama to an outfit, and Kate provides a perfect lesson in how to carry one off with aplomb ...

Angle it
All hats – but especially smaller, disc-shaped cocktail hats – should be worn at an angle. Kate always wears hers on the right side of her head.

Be age-appropriate
Larger hats are more suited to older women. Kate keeps her look young by choosing smaller hats that allow her to have her hair and face on show.

Limit other accessories
Remember, a hat is a dramatic statement. Don't go on to clutter your look with scarves and jewellery – opt instead for a streamlined look.

Keep hair simple
Your hairdo and your hat shouldn't be fighting for attention. By keeping her long hair in an everyday down style, Kate lets her hat do all the talking.

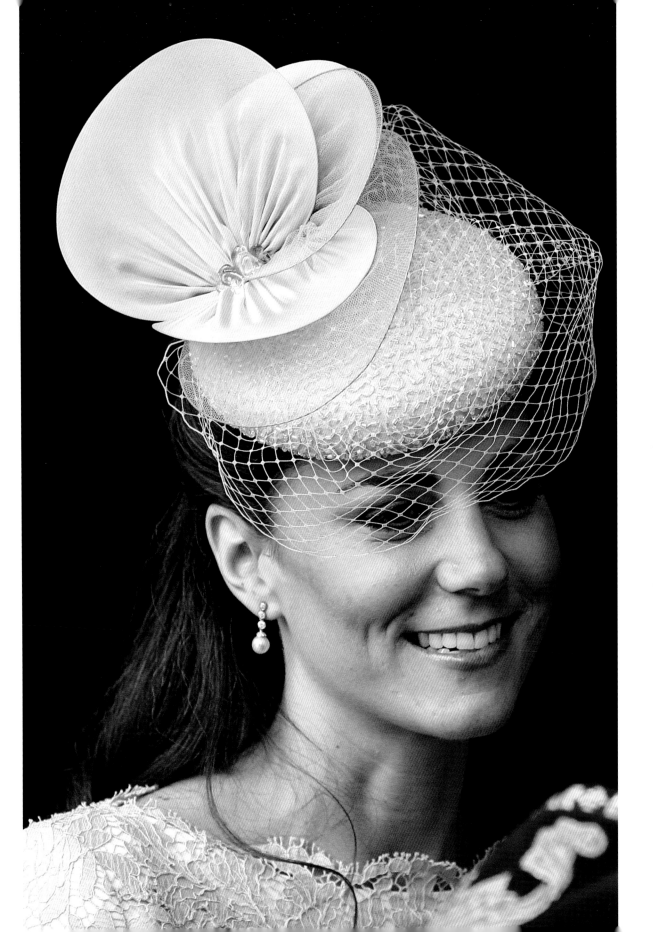

Checking Out in Style

The Dress For the launch of a new charitable scheme with Princes William and Harry on July 26, 2012 (the day before the start of the London Olympics), Kate aptly selected a simple Hobbs summer dress.

The three young Royals appeared at Bacon's College in Rotherhithe, southeast London, to launch the initiative of their charity, the Royal Foundation – a new programme that will train 16- to 19-year-olds to become qualified sports coaches and mentors. And with the Olympics just around the corner, Kate certainly took the gold medal when it came to chic summer style. The Duchess looked the picture of floaty perfection in a patterned white and grey checked linen frock. Its classic fit and flare silhouette suited her slender frame well, and also featured a modified boat-neck, short sleeves, full skirt and a concealed back zipper.

The dress is neatly cinched to show off her tiny waist with a striking white, African-inspired braided rope belt. Somewhat predictably, the remaining copies of the dress, which were already in the Hobbs sale for half price by the time Kate wore it, left stores in record time!

The Hair It's hard to tell from the photographs but the UK was in the middle of a heatwave, with temperatures of over 30°C (86°F), when Kate sported this immaculate blow-dry. No stranger to hot conditions following her official trips around the globe with William, the Duchess's hair remained perfectly in place, glossy and frizz-free – even when she played a quick game of football and refereed a judo match during the event!

The Shoes Kate finished off the look with her similarly purse-friendly, trusty "Imperia" wedges, from affordable high-street shoe store Pied à Terre – a shoe style that has been favoured by the Duchess on many other warm-weather occasions. This led fashion commentators at the *Daily Mail* newspaper to joke: "Forget the forecast, we Britons only truly know it's summer when the Duchess of Cambridge swaps her trusty L.K. Bennett 'Sledges' for a pair of Pied-à-Terre wedges." The espadrille-style wedges feature a canvas upper and buckle slingback and come in a range of colours, including the "natural" as worn here by Kate.

Make High-street Buys Heavenly

When Queen of the High Street Kate worked as a buyer for Jigsaw, she learnt exactly how careful picking from shops such as Zara, Warehouse and Hobbs results in lower-price bargains that can be made to look much more expensive. Here are some of her insider tricks …

Double up
Make like Kate and if you find a dress or top that you love and it's a fabulous fit, purchase the piece in two or more colours – at high-street prices, you can afford to!

Diffuse your look
Shopping on the high street doesn't have to mean giving designers a miss. An increasing number of Kate's favourite designers, such as Missoni and Alice Temperley, are extending their brands to provide a "diffusion" range – a cheaper version of their high-end fashion. Equally, some designers, such as Matthew Williamson with Debenhams, are now collaborating with high-street stores to provide catwalk-inspired pieces for a fraction of the cost.

Be fabric savvy
You don't have to skimp on the quality of clothes just because they are cheaper. Kate loves luxe fabrics such as silk and cashmere, which you can often find on the high street at a fraction of their high-end equivalent cost. Cheap fabrics look and feel inferior and will deteriorate very quickly, so check the label and stick to 100 per cent cotton, wool and silk.

Think high fashion
The high street is exactly the right place to experiment with new-season trends, cuts and colours. You can buy something edgy at an affordable price, which means you won't mind ditching it, if it looks dated by next year. Not that there's anything wrong with fashion recycling, of course – indeed, Kate is happy rewearing both the high-street and the designer pieces she loves.

Don't waste money on basics
As thrifty Kate knows, some basics simply aren't worth paying designer prices for. It makes sense to buy cheaper high-street versions of plain T-shirts, shirts and even jeans, depending on how long you expect them to last. Kate, for example, chooses more expensive denim brands such as J Brand for the navy jeans she wears frequently, but when experimenting with a bright electric-blue shade, she was happy to pick some up cheaply from Zara. Mixing high-street basics with stylish accessories quickly ups the apparent price tag of your overall look.

LOOK 25

Kate's Kane and Able

The Dress For a pre-Olympic reception at Buckingham Palace in June 2012, Kate wore this striking satin coat-dress, created for her by designer Christopher Kane. The formal, yet fashion-forward, frock was perfect for mingling with heads of state from all over the world, including the stylish US First Lady, Michelle Obama. The single-breasted design features sharp tailoring with streamlined darts, long sleeves, slanted pockets, a belted waist and peak lapels.

While the custom-made, ice-blue dress nodded to Kane's 2013 collection, it was in fact a softer, more demure take on the designer's edgy aesthetic, in keeping with Kate's signature style. Nevertheless, the designer, who won the New Establishment Award at the British Fashion Awards in 2011, was still an unexpected choice for the Duchess – not least to Kane himself.

Back in 2010, Scottish designer Kane had named Kate as one of the women he would love to design for and bemoaned the fact she was better known for wearing high-street pieces than for championing British designers: "It's a shame she doesn't wear more designers," he said at the time. "I don't really like the high street getting so much of the credit. I understand that there would be an array because you need to relate to so many people in the market, but she is a princess. If I were a princess, I'd be like, 'Oh yeah, bring it on!'"

Consequently, most fashion observers had written off Kane's chances of dressing the Duchess, as his pieces were considered to be too "out there" for Kate's more conservative, classic taste. But perhaps to prove that she doesn't always do the expected when it comes to style, she took up Kane's challenge and asked him to design a dress for her to wear to this very high-profile event when the world's media spotlight was sure to be focused on her outfit.

In fact, ever since the Royal Wedding, Kate's style confidence has continued to grow so that she has become far more open to experimentation when it comes to the more cutting-edge designers, trying, for example, Stella McCartney and Matthew Williamson for the first time. Perhaps most importantly, the beautiful coat-dress fitted her like a glove and proved to be a perfect choice for the occasion, combining fashion flair with understated elegance.

The Clutch Kate paired the coat-dress with a soft grey suede clutch by Alexander McQueen. The muted tones of the bag provide a great textural counterpoint to her shimmering dress.

McQueen's clutches usually feature a bold skull clasp. However, like Kate's dress, this piece was customized to work with her style, and the skull clasp was replaced with a simpler clasp. The fact that such high-profile designers are willing to alter their key pieces for Kate is further proof of how much sway she has over the fashion world.

The Earrings The Duchess's blue topaz and diamond earrings are by one of her favourite jewellery designers, Kiki McDonough. The hooped earrings have an open circle composed of 11 oval topazes, which graduate in size from top to bottom, creating an eye-catching effect.

Wearing Satin with Style

Satin is not a forgiving fabric. A badly made or poor-fitting piece in this shiny material is a glaringly obvious fashion disaster, which can make even the slimmest figure bulge in the wrong places. Yet Kate, as always, carries off this difficult look with ease, by following some important rules …

Fit is foremost
Any places in which the satin is pulled taut will be unflatteringly highlighted by the shiny fabric; even though Kate doesn't shy away from form-fitting numbers, on this occasion her dress is a little looser than usual. By opting for a more relaxed fit, she avoids any unwanted tight spots in the fabric. Sadly, most of us cannot buy bespoke so, if in doubt, go for a size up.

Keep it sleek
Excess fabric and swooshing A-line skirts can look bridal when cut in satin. Opt for sharp, tailored lines like Kate's coat-dress to keep the look sophisticated and occasion-appropriate. Always ensure satin is perfectly pressed to avoid unflattering folds or creases.

Smarten it up
By going for a coat-dress rather than her classic shift or sheath-style dress, Kate cleverly mixes masculine tailoring with feminine fabric, preventing the look from becoming prissy.

Consider what lies beneath
Choice of underwear is also very important when wearing satin, and Kate would never dream of being spotted with something so vulgar as a VPL (visible pantie line). Invest in a set of flesh-coloured seamless panties and bra to avoid satin draping awkwardly over lacy lingerie or bulky seams.

Stylish Olympic Spirit

The Dress While cheering on Andy Murray at the Olympic Men's Singles Quarter-finals on August 2, 2012, Kate wore a Stella McCartney "Ridley Stretch Cady" dress, which she'd previously worn to an Olympics exhibition at the National Portrait Gallery, just two weeks earlier. This simple crepe shift embodies classic luxury with its figure-hugging minimalist silhouette and eye-catching royal blue hue.

McCartney was also the British designer chosen to create the official Olympic kit for Team GB for London 2012, so the dress made a perfect choice for the team's most photographed supporter. For her Olympic kit, McCartney famously played down the red of the traditional Union Jack flag and instead accented the blue – "something that was very important to me was to try and use that very iconic image but to dismantle it and try to soften it, break it down and make it more fashionable in a sense", said the designer at the time. Kate is so cute with fashion that it is probably no coincidence that she was seen sporting a bold blue Stella McCartney for two key Olympic events. With this smart colour choice, she proudly shows her support for the British designer and her patriotic solidarity with the British athletes, wearing McCartney's blue outfits.

Kate and Prince William also caused a stir on this occasion in choosing to sit among the crowd instead of using Wimbledon's famous Royal Box. Foregoing special privileges at an important event is another clear signal that the pair are keen to be seen as a very modern couple who can mix formal and informal, and enjoy themselves, whatever the surroundings.

The Blazer Kate topped her dress with a tailored, one-button blazer from the Canadian label Smythe Les Vestes. Known for their perfectly tailored and sartorially savvy blazers, Smythe have acquired a strong cult following among celebrities and fashion editors alike. The blazer's bold gold buttons, large lapels, masculine tailoring and cutout back panel give this classic item a contemporary flair.

It was, in fact, the third time Kate wore this navy blazer to Olympic events in a week, but then the Duchess has made an art of picking versatile pieces, in classic shapes, that work perfectly with the rest of her wardrobe to create a number of different looks. It is this knack of selecting hard-working pieces that can be used in multiple ways that has earned Kate the title "Queen of the Capsule Wardrobe" among some of her adoring fashion press.

The Clutch Kate matched her navy blazer with a navy suede "Muse" clutch bag from Russell & Bromley. The piece was designed by Stuart Weitzman, another favourite of the Duchess when it comes to accessories, and a label that also counts both singer Beyoncé and actress Angelina Jolie as fans.

The Shoes Another clear favourite during the Olympics were the Stuart Weitzman "Coco Pop" shoes. The fact that this comfortable pair hardly left the Duchess's feet during the Games was not lost on Weitzman. "She didn't change her shoes for nine days. It was a big deal!" he delightedly observed. Predictably, the Coco Pop's stacked style became an instant hit.

The Sunglasses Throughout the tense match, Kate protected her eyes from the sunlight with a pair of sleek Givenchy SGV 761 sunglasses. Featuring broad arms and rectangular frames, the glasses oozed simple French chic.

Speak Volumes with Your Fashion Choices

Don't be fooled by her effortlessly stylish appearance, Kate puts an incredible amount of thought into everything she wears. Even a seemingly simple outfit such as her vibrant blue dress and navy blazer combo actually makes a discrete statement about the event she is attending. In paying attention to these key details, Kate ensures her outfit is always on message.

Match your designer to your destination
Think about where you've bought your clothes. Picking a piece by a designer who has ties with the event or the location that you will be visiting, as Kate has done with her McCartney dress, is a cute sartorial nod that won't be lost on seasoned fashion-watchers.

Symbolize with accessories
You don't have to wear official or sponsored pieces to show your support for an event. Think outside the box and look for accessories that play on themes of the day. Kate first paired her McCartney dress with a circular pendant necklace by Cartier, and often sported her circular Kiki McDonough earrings during her appearances at the Games, choices that cleverly played on the Olympic Rings in a high-fashion way.

Insider jokes
Kate loves making clever sartorial statements, which only true fashion insiders will notice. Another example of this is on Look 15 (see page 73) when Kate wore shoes named after a type of daffodil for St David's Day. These little details are the sign of a true fashionista, who thinks about what she wears and is confident enough to let her outfits do the talking.

Show your true colours
Throughout the Olympics, Kate dressed in blue, paying homage to the uniforms of her home team.

Flying the Flag for British Fashion

The Dress For her appearance at the London 2012 Olympic Games Closing Ceremony on August 12, 2012, Kate chose to wear the same dress she had worn to the Diamond Jubilee Concert in June. It was fitting, and typically clever, for the Duchess to sartorially tie together the two events that effectively served as the bookends for what was an especially golden summer for the UK.

The long-sleeved bodycon dress is from one of Kate's favourite high-street brands, Whistles. Although the so-called "Bella" dress may have been off the peg, it could have been designed especially for Kate, as it perfectly fits not only her slender frame but also her signature demure style. The aqua colouring was a great way to round off Kate's Olympic run of "blue outfits", while the multi-petal print provides a fun edge – perfect for such a jubilant occasion. She chose to accentuate the dress's flattering nipped-in waist and ruching detail with the addition of a thin black belt.

Kate has become something of an unofficial ambassador for the Whistles label, with her support of the brand causing the company website to crash when avid followers frantically fought to log on! But even Whistles, which had plenty of previous experience of the "Kate Effect", were surprised by just how huge the response was to this global televised event. "The biggest impact has been on a dress she wore at the Closing Ceremony," confirmed Jane Shepherdson, chief executive of Whistles: "It's a style that's been very successful for us anyway – a printed silk dress. That weekend, we sold out of it."

The Olympics Closing Ceremony celebrated home-grown talent, from sporting to artistic, including a segment featuring famous British models such as Kate Moss, Lily Cole and Naomi Campbell in extravagant outfits from British designers, including Erdem, Victoria Beckham and Alexander McQueen. Kate is always keen to fly the flag for British fashion, and her made-in-Britain outfit was perfectly in keeping with the theme of the occasion, while also juxtaposing the show's couture fashion with more accessible pieces.

The Earrings As at the Diamond Jubilee Concert, Kate echoed the colour of her dress with blue topaz and diamond earrings by Kiki McDonough, the same pair she wore in June. These circular earrings cleverly pick up on the design of the Olympic rings, a little fashion in-joke that explains why Kate wore this pair to so many of her Olympic appearances.

The Arm Candy Kate completed this recycled outfit with her trusty white gold Tiffany "Diamond's by the Yard" bracelet and her Anya Hindmarch "Maud" clutch. Crafted of soft satin and made using tightly woven thread, the black clutch has a luxurious glossy appearance.

Dressing Up High-street Buys

While designer pieces were being flaunted during the Closing Ceremony, Kate ensured her high-street dress held its own amid all the finery by using some simple style tricks …

Add embellishments
Designer pieces tend to have more detail than high-street pieces but by simply wearing a slim black belt with her dress, Kate adds another note of visual interest.

Savvy sizing
Don't always stick to the same-size clothing. Pick pieces that fit you like a glove, no matter what the size says on the label, and you'll look as if it was especially made for you. Searching for the perfect fit, rather than an ideal size, ensures Kate's Whistles dress looks every bit as special as the pieces that she has custom-made.

Wear striking jewellery
Kate's pretty earrings caught the light whenever she moved her head, adding a little edge and flair to an otherwise simple outfit.

Pick a print
The right print can add a twist to any outfit and can also have the effect of making a piece appear more expensive. The tight-petal print on the Whistles dress is more impressionistic than classic floral and, consequently, brings the look bang up-to-date.

A Rare and Exotic Bloom

The Dress When Kate and Prince William arrived in Singapore on September 12, 2012, for a visit to the island's Botanical Gardens on the first day of their royal tour of Southeast Asia and the South Pacific, all eyes were drawn to the Duchess's exquisite pastel-pink, kimono-style dress. The royal couple were there to see the *Vanda* William Catherine orchid, a newly created orchid named in their honour. And what better way to dress for this special occasion than by choosing a special orchid-print dress?

The stunning silk dress, made for Kate by British designer Jenny Packham, was covered in tiny orchids, which took a team of skilled artists at Chelsea firm de Gournay eight weeks to hand paint. The knee-grazing number also had three-quarter sleeves, a deep V-neck and a full skirt, and was cinched in at the waist to hug Kate's delicate contours. "She looked beautiful and we are all very proud," the team at Packham declared. Even Prince William himself remarked that the colours of the hybrid *Vanda* William Catherine orchid perfectly matched the Duchess's dress – another example of Kate's amazing attention to detail when selecting an outfit.

Jenny Packham does not sell any of the designs she has made especially for the Duchess, frustrating Kate's most avid fashion followers, but this ensures that the bespoke outfits remain that extra bit special. "We're not Reiss," explained Packham in a good-humoured aside. Indeed, the designer's flagship boutique, on the site of a former bank in Mayfair, London, is visited by only a privileged few, and feels anything but high street. The extremely private dressing room, where clients, including Kate Winslet, Elizabeth Hurley and Angelina Jolie, slip on their bespoke clothes, is a windowless space inside a former vault.

While visiting the gardens, Kate and William were also shown a white orchid, named after William's late mother, Diana. The Princess of Wales had been delighted to have a flower named in her honour, but tragically died in a Paris car crash just two weeks before she was due to fly out to see it for herself.

The Shoes and Bag Instead of her usual nude heels, Kate sported a pair of off-white "Park Avenue" courts from Russell & Bromley, and carried a matching "Park Avenue" clutch. Although nude-toned shoes would have worked well with this dress, after a 14-hour flight, head-to-toe flesh tones might have caused Kate to look washed-out, whereas

Vanda William Catherine

her off-white shoes picked up on the off-white detailing in the floral dress and helped to ensure the Duchess looked as fresh as a daisy.

The Earrings Kate's 18-carat gold earrings are "Classic Baroque Pearl Earring Drops" from Annoushka Jewellery, the eponymous line from Annoushka Ducas, who also founded another of Kate's go-to jewellery collections, Links of London, in the 1990s. "I am so thrilled to see the Duchess of Cambridge wearing my favourite pearl drop earrings on so many occasions," said Ducas.

The Hair Kate might have just endured a long-haul flight before visiting the Botanical Gardens, but her hair betrayed no sign of fatigue! As always, her glossy locks looked perfectly groomed – neatly pinned back at the sides and front, but worn loose in cascading curls at the back. Taking some of the credit for this was Amanda Cook Tucker, the new hairstylist Kate took along with her for this official tour of Southeast Asia. Cook Tucker has cut William and Harry's hair since they were children and while Kate still goes to Richard Ward's salon in London's Chelsea, she occasionally likes to have her hair done at home and to have a stylist who will happily travel abroad. Cook Tucker proved indispensable on this trip, during which Kate had to contend with the implacable enemy of smooth hair – hot, humid weather. But Palace insiders were quick to reveal that the British taxpayer wasn't footing this particular grooming bill. Instead, the Prince of Wales paid the hairdresser's estimated £300-a-day ($486) fees plus travel costs.

Capture a Sense of Occasion in Your Clothes

Kate's clothes don't just match her shoes, they match the occasion, too. Here's how you can capture the essence of an event in your own outfits ...

Highlight the key detail
With her specially created orchid-print dress, Kate is paying homage to the reason for her visit to Singapore's Botanical Gardens. She could have settled for a floral pattern but by going one step further and selecting an orchid pattern in the same shade as the flower named after her, she really captures the spirit of the event.

Pay respect to your hosts
If the pattern pays tribute to the flower, the oriental style of Kate's dress is a respectful nod to Singapore's fashion history and to the influence it has had on designers around the world.

Keeping the fairytale alive
The neckline and sleeves of this dress were similar to Kate's famous Alexander McQueen wedding gown. By picking up details from such an important dress, Kate is carefully crafting her own personal fashion narrative and placing the newly created orchid inside her own romantic history.

Kate Goes Graphic

The Dress She may love home-grown talent, but Kate proved she had a finger on the international fashion pulse when she stepped out in this eye-catching yet elegant dress by Singapore-born designer Prabal Gurung, to attend a state dinner hosted by the President of Singapore, on September 11, 2012.

The unusual purple and cream floral printed wool-silk dress, from the designer's Spring/Summer 2012 collection, was inspired by a series of photographs titled "Sensual Flowers" by the renowned Japanese artist Nobuyoshi Araki. Prints were arranged symmetrically down the front of the dresses, with the reverse patterns matching up in an undulating design. Kate's dress is knee-length, with a bateau neckline, three-quarter sleeves, a concealed zipper and a classic shift silhouette.

Since launching his label in New York in 2009, Gurung has gathered a long list of celebrity clients, including Michelle Obama and Sarah Jessica Parker, yet he was very excited when he learned that the Duchess of Cambridge was wearing one of his pieces, especially in his home country of Singapore. "This is the ultimate honour," he declared. "I had been hoping that she would wear one of our dresses but for it to happen while she's visiting the part of the world I was born in and right in the midst of New York Fashion Week is an absolute dream come true."

The designer also took to Twitter to express his joy, telling his followers how he was so excited that he "stopped some strangers on the street" to show them a picture of "Kate Middleton in our dress!".

The Accessories Not for the first time has Kate let her bold choice of dress do all the talking, finishing off her look with a selection of accessories that she has been seen with many times before: her Anya Hindmarch "Maud" clutch, black Prada satin heels and a glittering diamond bracelet, believed to have been a wedding present and which she previously wore to a BAFTA dinner (see also page 63).

Grab Attention in Graphic Prints

If you're undecided about donning a "look-at-me" print, follow these tips for pulling off bold fabric designs with all the classical elegance of Kate …

Rule of thumb
Small, intricate prints are better for making you appear smaller, while larger patterns usually make you look, well, larger.

Balance it out
When wearing a graphic print dress, keep accessories neutral, and hair and make-up clean and simple, to avoid the look becoming too busy.

Focus attention where you want it
Remember, eyes will be drawn to bold prints, so think carefully about their placement. If you have a boyish frame, go for prints that fall on the bust and hips, and if you are curvier, look for prints that draw the eye to the centre of the outfit.

Be sensible with shapes
The sleek, sophisticated shape of Kate's classic shift ensures her overall look is chic and not gaudy.

LOOK 30

Kate Pays Her Respects

The Dress Kate wore another bespoke Jenny Packham creation when she and William paid a moving visit to Singapore's Kranji War Memorial, which bears the names of more than 24,000 Commonwealth casualties from the Second World War.

At the foot of the memorial, the royal couple laid a beautiful wreath of red roses, white lilies and orchids on behalf of the Queen and Prince Philip, with the accompanying message: "In Memory of the Glorious Dead, Elizabeth R and Philip".

Fitting for the solemn occasion on which she was representing HM the Queen herself, Kate's dress was a soft, tranquil colour – the same "duck-egg blue" shade that featured heavily in Jenny Packham's Spring 2011 collection. However, as with all Packham's creations for the Duchess, this graceful shirt-dress, featuring three-quarter length sleeves, button-front bodice, lace overlay, nipped-in waist and pleated knee-length skirt, was custom-made to suit the Duchess's now signature look.

The Shoes A visit to a cemetery is not an occasion for look-at-me shoes and once again Kate put her trust in her nude patent L.K. Bennett "Sledge" pumps. She may have faced some criticism for wearing the same pair of shoes on so many different occasions but her knack for creating clever capsule collections for foreign trips is built on versatile pieces that can be mixed and matched. Few items work as hard as these courts – the perfect neutral anchor for a great variety of colourful outfits.

The Parasol Keeping accessories to a bare minimum for this sombre event, Kate chose to protect her skin and hair from the midday heat with a paper parasol. Despite looking fittingly Far Eastern, she had actually bought it from a small family-run business based in East Calder, Scotland.

Christine Naysmith runs Brolliesgalore with her mum Linda, and the pair have been selling bespoke umbrellas online since 2003. They received a surprising call for a rush order on the paper and bamboo "Sa" parasol just before Kate left for the Orient.

"I couldn't believe it when I picked up the phone and it was a girl from Clarence House, asking about the parasol," recalled Christine excitedly. "She wanted the cream-coloured one and explained it was for the Duchess and she needed it quickly because she was going on tour, so we had it sent by courier."

The family received an even bigger shock when their creation appeared on the news. "I was cooking tea when my daughter Christine shouted me through from the front room and the Duchess was on the TV, holding our umbrella," mum Linda explained. "Everyone was jumping up and down and we phoned everyone that works for us."

The cause of all this celebration is a delicate white paper parasol with panels handmade from the bark of the mulberry tree, and a 60-cm (24 in) bamboo stem with a carved handle made from sustainable wood.

Look Pretty in Pleats

For many women, pleats bring back memories of unflattering school uniforms, but pleated skirts have become one of Kate's fail-safe style choices. She has modelled versions from designers including Jenny Packham, Alexander McQueen and Jaeger, and somehow her classic look and perfect posture ensure they always appear sophisticated and chic. Here's how to follow her lead in pleats ...

Look out for length
Too short and you'll look like a schoolgirl, too long and you'll appear matronly. Kate gets it just right by picking skirts that fall on, or just above, the knee.

Smooth lines
Too tight and the pleats won't fall right, and will look messy and uneven. For a more flattering effect, pleats should lie flat. If you have curvy hips and thighs, don't bypass a pleated skirt; just look for skinny "accordion" pleats – thin pleats are more elongating.

Lighten up
Pleats made out of thick, heavy fabric can add excess volume to your lower half and make you look dumpy. However, lighter fabrics have none of this heaviness and stiffness – instead, they lightly skim the body, creating a delicate sense of fullness.

Perfect proportions
High-waisted full pleats, as featured in Kate's Jenny Packham frock, add a couple of extra inches to your lower half and will balance out the volume of the skirt to create a flattering, leg-lengthening effect.

LOOK 31

Modest Mosque Magic

The Dress A visit to a mosque, complete with rigid dress code, is an engagement that could trip up many fashionistas, but Kate appeared cool, calm and collected in this pretty pale mint Beulah London "Sabitri" dress and matching headscarf when she and William called in at the As Syakirin Mosque in Kuala Lumpur on September 14, 2012.

The Duchess had clearly put a lot of time and thought into her choice of clothing for such a culturally sensitive occasion and settled on this respectful but still beautiful silk chiffon combination. In covering her hair and arms and wearing a below-the-knee dress, Kate displayed full respect for Islamic religious protocols, yet the dress still offered a shapely silhouette. Demure but distinctly feminine, the soft hue shades perfectly suited her brunette colouring, too.

Royal commentators were quick to point out that this highly appropriate outfit evoked memories of Princess Diana, who displayed similar fashion savvy on multiple royal visits to mosques. In particular, Kate's late mother-in-law appeared in a very similar outfit on a visit to a mosque during a tour of Egypt in 1992.

The Duchess's choice of designer was Beulah London, a label she has previously worn – including stepping out in their coral and white flower-patterned "Blossom" dress for a friend's Somerset wedding in June 2012. This particular dress is actually a bespoke version of the same "Blossom" design, with an almost identical shape and cut. Ethical fashion brand Beulah London is owned by a friend of Kate and William, Lady Natasha Rufus Isaacs, and is dedicated to social justice, including employing former victims of Indian human trafficking to help manufacture clothing and accessories.

Founded in 2011, the brand has already won many high-profile customers, including Kate Moss, Sienna Miller, Sarah Jessica Parker and Demi Moore. And yet this much-photographed occasion was perhaps Beulah London's largest showcase so far. The morning after the Duchess wore this pretty dress, the label was inundated with requests from women all over the world, desperate to get their hands on it. Only Kate could transform what was a sensitive diplomatic visit into fashion frenzy, without ever looking as if she was trying too hard.

The Bag Kate's clutch was the suitably modest and also much-loved beige L.K. Bennett "Natalie", which made regular appearances on the 2011 royal tour of Canada and has continued to be a versatile favourite.

The Shoes Kate wore her ever-faithful L.K. Bennett nude "Sledge" pumps with this pale dress but, in accordance with Islamic practices, she removed her shoes to enter the mosque, revealing the trademark nude tights she was wearing underneath. Ever a keen observer of important details, her toenails were not painted, as it is deemed inappropriate for a woman to wear any nail varnish when entering a mosque.

Be Bold with Your Brows

Wearing a headscarf was, of course, part of the dress code for the mosque, but on this particular occasion it drew even more attention to Kate's face and her choice of tastefully natural make-up. It also made a feature of her perfectly groomed eyebrows. Indeed, Kate's straight, full, defined brows have become something of a trademark look for the Duchess and she has been credited with starting a new trend for bolder, bushier shapes, as opposed to very thin or arched styles. Here's how you, too, can achieve statement brows that frame your face in the most flattering way ...

Establish a good base shape
Brows should start in line with the corner of your eye. To work out where they should finish, line up a make-up brush at a diagonal angle running from the corner of your nose along the outside of your iris as you look forward. Your brow should end at the point crossing the line of the brush.

Fake the fullness
Kate's secret weapon is reported to be Bobbi Brown eyeshadow powder in "Sable". Use a slanted eyeshadow brush to apply a colour two shades darker than your hair to fill in any gaps in your brows.

Try a dye job
Having your eyebrows professionally dyed at a beauty salon is a great way to add Kate-style definition.

Keep them tidy
Kate's brows never have a hair out of place. Use an eyebrow brush or a clean mascara brush to groom unruly hairs into shape, and set them with a slick of Vaseline.

Kate's Malaysian Marvel

The Dress Glittering in gold and soft white, Kate dazzled in a floor-length Alexander McQueen gown as she attended a lavish dinner thrown by the Malaysian head of state, Sultan Abdul Halim of Kedah, at the opulent Istana Negara state palace in Kuala Lumpur.

The dress featured a fitted bodice and a flared skirt, which flowed out from the empire waistline, with gold lamé embroidery bordering the sleeves, neck and centre of the gown. Her sweetheart neckline caused some murmurs from onlookers as to its appropriateness in a conservative country, however Kate kept the tops of her arms covered and wore a floor-skimming skirt in line with local protocol.

As is customary with Kate's bespoke pieces, there is more to this creation than what first meets the eye: scattered over the fabric was glittering gold lamé embroidery in a hibiscus motif. The hibiscus is the official flower of Malaysia, making this subtle design detail another example of the Duchess's canny ability to pay homage to her host country through her choice of outfit.

The Jewellery Kate picked up on the hibiscus print of her dress with her leaf-shaped gold jewellery. The "Double Leaf" earrings and matching "Spread Your Wings (Scale)" bracelet are by designer Catherine Zoraida, who is known for her exquisitely handcrafted pieces. Born in Colombia but raised in Scotland, Zoraida says she combines the influences of both countries in her nature-inspired designs. Featuring beautifully engraved feather details, both of these gold-plated silver items were handmade in England.

The Duchess picked out the pieces from myflashtrash.com, a jewellery store founded by *Made in Chelsea* TV star Amber Atherton. The company's head of PR, Abbey Keys, commented: "Kate can't accept gifting, so for our

designers it's a lovely feeling to know that she has chosen these pieces because she genuinely likes them, instead of just wearing them because they were a gift."

The Bag The clutch carried by Kate is one that she has used for many formal events, as has her sister Pippa, who owns a matching one. The shiny gold purse, with a dramatic jewel-encrusted brooch clasp, is from Wilbur & Gussie – a label founded by childhood friends Brett Tyne and Lucy Lyons. "Wilbur and Gussie were our family pets when we were growing up, and therefore integral parts of our childhood," the pair explained. "Naming our business proved to be no easy task, until we came up with the idea to incorporate their names. Regal mongrel cat Wilbur reflects what's elegant and refined about us, and Gussie, the strong-minded Westie dog, mirrors what's bold and occasionally off-the-wall."

Interest in the then relatively unknown brand's "Charlie" clutch bag rocketed when the Duchess of Cambridge was pictured carrying the glittering envelope design. The bag itself is also named after a pet – a blue Burmese cat. "He's a bit of a show-stopper due to his striking good looks, but not inherently an attention-seeker," they explained. "He's quietly confident and head-turningly handsome."

The Shoes Just peeping out from the bottom of Kate's skirt were Jimmy Choo "Dart Glitter" sandals in gold. They may be hidden but the high heels and platforms on these shoes helped balance out the proportions of Kate's floor-length gown and gave her the necessary added height to carry off such a flowing shape.

Pick Out a Show-stopping Outfit

The eyes of the fashion world are always on Kate – even when she's just in a sweater and jeans. Yet she still knows how to pull out all the stops and wow a crowd when a more formal occasion calls for it. Here's how she does it ...

Step out of your comfort zone
Kate usually wears shift dresses to formal events, with waists that fall on the natural waistline. In going for a full-length empire-line outfit, so markedly different from her normal choices, she knows that she will set tongues wagging for all the right reasons.

Go for gold
Train the spotlight on yourself by wearing metallics. They glitter and shine in the evening lights, and instantly add spectacle and sparkle.

Create a dramatic silhouette
Whether it's a billowing ballgown or an elaborate bell-shaped sleeve, creating a striking silhouette ensures you will stand out from the crowd and look dramatic in photos.

Play with proportion
The empire-line cut of Kate's dress makes it look as if she has legs that literally go all the way up to her armpits! A grand occasion such as this is the perfect opportunity to display your best assets to the max.

OPPOSITE: It had been rumoured that the Duchess of Cambridge would wear a tiara for this official state dinner at Istana Negara Palace in Kuala Lumpur, but she chose to keep things simple instead. Her brunette locks were partially pulled back and up at the sides and front, then loosely twisted into place at the back, with the rest of her long hair falling in a soft waterfall of cascading curls.

A Vision of Grace in Lace

The Dress When she attended the Diamond Jubilee tea party hosted by the British High Commissioner at his residence in Kuala Lumpur on September 14, 2012, Kate chose to wear this delightful ice-blue dress with white lace overlay by one of her all-time favourite British designers, Alice Temperley. Lace is, of course, the perfect choice for afternoon tea, and Kate looked cool and chic in the outfit, despite this marking what must have been one of the most difficult days for the Duchess of Cambridge since she first became a public figure. Only that morning, she had been informed that unauthorized pictures of her sunbathing while topless on holiday had been published by the French magazine *Closer*. And yet this emerging scandal didn't prevent unflappable Kate from looking calm and elegant and smiling charmingly for the waiting photographers.

Her knee-length dress with three-quarter sheer sleeves, a boat neckline and flared skirt is a modified version of the "Aster Flower Dress" from Temperley London's Autumn/Winter 2012 collection. The original frock came in black silk with a gold overlay, but the designer created this pale blue and white version especially for Kate, as the lighter palette was more fitting for the tropical climate on her royal tour of Southeast Asia and the South Pacific.

Alice Temperley has seen her designs worn by both Middleton sisters, a boost that is not lost on the designer.

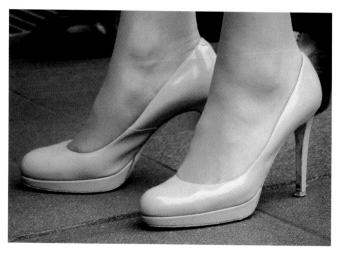

"Awareness is good for any brand," she has admitted. "They're wonderful girls to dress and wonderful girls to be around, so I think it's all flattering." The Somerset-born designer also said of Kate: "She's been brilliant for British fashion and great for the whole economy. There is no one else who has an effect like her. It has really brought British fashion to the forefront again. She is a breath of fresh air and has encouraged people to experiment and combine high fashion with high-street fashion. She is a really nice girl as well."

The Hairpins Kate wore her hair in an elaborate plaited chignon decorated with pearl pins. The style was another subtle nod of respect to the culture of her host country, as Malay women frequently wear pearl pins in their hair, especially at weddings.

The Shoes Once again, Kate's feet were cushioned in her trusty nude L.K. Bennett "Sledge" courts.

The Earrings The Duchess's earrings, by an unnamed designer, comprised a line of five diamonds from which suspends a teardrop consisting of a large blue stone encircled by more diamonds.

ABOVE: As exemplified in this picture, Kate, who prefers to do her own make-up, has become a master at cleverly defining her eyes. One of her secrets is that she often uses navy or dark brown mascara rather than jet-black, to create a softer look. She is also never seen without eyeliner, usually lining the whole eye but, again to avoid a harsh finish, she tends to choose charcoal-grey or dark brown rather than black.

Wear Lace Well

Kate is clearly a huge fan of lace designs. In fact, ever since she chose a wedding dress featuring a bodice of French Chantilly lace and English Cluny lace, the Duchess has returned to the fabric for many of her public appearances. If a collection of one of Kate's favourite designers, from Erdem to Temperley, features a lace dress, you can be sure she will snap up a version of it. But it can still be a tricky fabric to wear well, so here's how to ensure you look elegant and ladylike in lace ...

Tailoring and lace combination
Sharp, tailored shapes are the perfect counterbalance to lace's whimsical flimsiness. Keeping edges clean, as seen in Kate's Alexander McQueen shift featured in Look 23 (see page 100), prevents lace from appearing tacky or twee.

Experiment with colours
The delicate, sheer nature of the fabric means you can get away with wearing lace in colours that you may usually find draining, especially if there is a contrasting or deeper-coloured underlay fabric.

Don't slip up
Lace creates an effect that is subtly sexy. Keep the look classy, not trashy, by ensuring you wear a full slip underneath. A VPL (visible panty line) and visible bra straps are so unladylike!

Too much of a good thing
One lace piece is enough! Matching a lace dress with a lace shawl, gloves or other accessories is simply overkill.

Let lower layers shine through
Experiment with different colour slips underneath a lace top or dress to create entirely different outfits. Soft pastel colours, as in Kate's Temperley dress, play up to the pretty romantic nature of the fabric, while jewel-bright colours underneath can create a more dramatic, gothic effect.

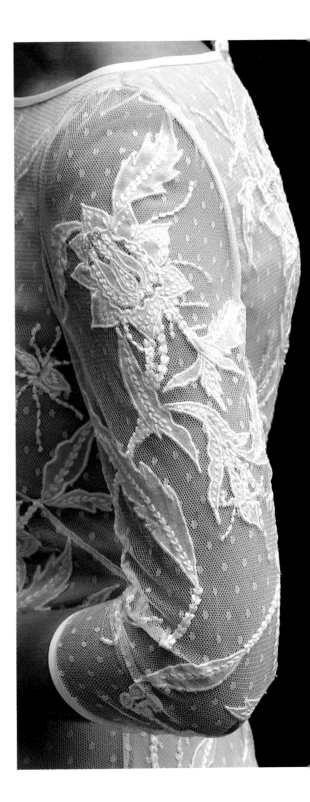

LOOK 34

Aussie Fashion Rules

The Dress It is surely no coincidence that the first time Kate stepped foot on Australian soil was also the first time she wore a piece by the Project D label. Although the brand is based in London, the more famous half of the designer duo behind it is Aussie popstar Dannii Minogue. She set up the label with her best friend, Tabitha Somerset Webb, in 2010. In just a few short years, Project D has gained popularity for its range of gorgeous frocks, including chic cocktail dresses, red-carpet glamour gowns and super-stylish day numbers.

Kate wore the "Penelope" dress in pale powder-pink from Project D's Spring/Summer 2012 collection, which features a fold-down collar, cuffed short sleeves, box-pleated skirt, waist tie, thin belt loops and an invisible zipper on the front. The simple tea dress was made out of lightweight silk crepe de Chine, making it well suited to the climate of both the Polynesian island Tuvalu, from where the couple flew, and Brisbane, Australia, where they landed.

Kate's sister, Pippa Middleton, had previously worn a Project D "Phoebe Bluebird Peplum" dress back in July of the same year to watch the tennis at Wimbledon, but it was when the Duchess was snapped in the "Penelope" dress that the small-scale brand, with a total staff of just 11, was suddenly front-page news.

"I was getting onto a flight back to Australia, just about to turn off my phone when a text came through saying she was wearing one of our dresses," recalled an elated Dannii Minogue. "There are actually only four left now on the rack in the office."

Getting Kate into one of their girlie, sassy frocks was a personal victory for Minogue, who had confessed to reporters back in March: "There's probably not a brand in town that wouldn't want to dress the Duchess of Cambridge. She's an iconic, gorgeous girl and if she ever chose to wear Project D, we would be incredibly proud."

The Shoes During their journey back to the UK from the Far East on September 19, 2012, the Duke and Duchess of Cambridge had a two-hour stopover at Brisbane Airport, and Kate ensured she was comfortable for the occasion by slipping into her well-worn L.K. Bennett nude "Sledge" pumps.

The Earrings Kate also chose this occasion to showcase a new pair of earrings – the 24-carat gold-plated disc stud earrings with a pale blue amazonite drop were another delightful high-street discovery. The brand is called Azuni and it is widely available from John Lewis.

Azuni's founder and designer, Ashley Marshall, actually began his career as a chef, working in some of London's top kitchens, such as the Dorchester hotel, The Ivy and Le Caprice, before spending time living in South America, where he picked up the cultural influences clearly seen in his work. Marshall likes to experiment with unusual textures and stones to create jewellery that sits "Between Two Worlds", such as these antique-style earrings.

OPPOSITE: When leaving the Polynesian island Tuvalu to head back to Britain, Kate and Prince William were taken to their plane on a throne lifted by local men, escorted by colourful dancers, and were presented with these traditional floral head garlands. As always, Kate anticipates this honour by wearing a silk flower-print Project D dress that perfectly complements the flower "crown", known locally as a *fou*.

Picking the Right Celebrity Designers

Kate may be a fan of Danni Minogue's label Project D, but she is choosy about which celebrity designers receive the royal seal of approval. Here is how she always makes the right decision ...

Choose for yourself

Recently, Kate returned a collection of clothes sent to her from the range created for Dorothy Perkins by the famous American Kardashian sisters. A representative of the Duchess noted at the time: "In general terms, the policy of the Duke and Duchess of Cambridge is not to accept any unsolicited gifts unless the sender is known personally to His or Her Royal Highness. Any such gifts are returned to the sender with thanks and an explanation of Their Royal Highnesses' policy."

Stick to your signature style

Although Kate cannot accept gifts, if there had been a piece in the Kardashian collection that caught her eye, she would probably have bought it. But the racy collection featuring a lot of animal prints – which Dorothy Perkins dubbed the Kardashians' "look at me" red-carpet glamour – is a far cry from Kate's more demure, classic style.

Try before you buy

Just because you admire a celebrity's personal style doesn't mean their clothes will work on you. Kate asked to be sent a selection from Victoria Beckham's highly successful Spring/Summer 2011 collection, as favoured by many Hollywood A-listers. However, to date she has never worn anything from the range, suggesting that after trying on the off-the-peg pieces, she decided they simply didn't work for her.

Keeping Out the Cold

The Coat For the opening of St George's Park, the Football Association's new National Football Centre in Staffordshire, on October 9, 2012, Kate wore this "Angel Fit and Flare" coat in a flattering shade of khaki-green from her much-favoured British high-street brand Reiss.

The wool coat, from the Reiss Autumn/Winter 2010 collection, is very much aligned with Kate's signature look: elegant tailoring, which nips in at the waist before flaring out into a full skirt. The knee-length coat also features large cuffs, a hidden front fastening and a wide funnel collar, which can be turned up (as Kate did) or worn folded down.

The popular high-street store first opened in 1971 and, in more recent years, has gained a reputation for design-led, directional clothing that is especially popular with young, city-based professionals who want affordable smart fashion with a bit of catwalk edge. The brand has been one of the few British retailers to crack the American market after opening its first store in Greenwich Village, New York, in 2005.

Kate actually purchased her coat from the Reiss outlet store, which sells surplus stock from previous collections at cheaper prices and is based at her favourite cut-price shopping centre: Bicester Village in Oxfordshire. Ever the style recycler, she had previously worn it on Christmas Day 2011 at Sandringham, when on her way to a church service with the Princesses Beatrice and Eugenie.

The Belt Kate ensured her simple coat looked dressed up enough for the formal occasion with the addition of a statement belt that cinched the coat in extra-tight at the waist. The black patent mock-croc "Betony" belt is also from Reiss, but from their 2009 collection. In mixing and matching pieces from different seasons, Kate is showing off another aspect of her keen fashion eye, creating timeless looks from favourite saved pieces, rather than blindly following current seasonal trends.

The Boots For the footie-flavoured event, Kate picked her favourite boots – the Aquatalia "Rhumba" – and teamed them with opaque black tights. It's not always advisable to wear heels on grass, but the low heel didn't cause her any problems. Although the weatherproofed suede and slip-resistant rubber sole proved suitable attire for a pitch inspection, sporty Kate still joked about slipping into something more suitable for a kickabout. She gamely responded to the joke from Burton MP Andrew Griffiths about joining in the action with: "Have you got a pair of trainers I can borrow?"

Belt Up! - the Five Belts Every Girl Needs

Kate is a dedicated fan of waist belts and has a collection of classic styles that she uses to alter many different outfits. With just a handful of belts at your disposal, you can transform the look of simple dresses, coats and top-and-skirt combinations. Your essential waist belt collection should consist of the following ...

The skinny belt
Perfect for drawing the eye to the narrowest point on your figure, skinny belts look best worn with delicate fabrics, such as lace or fine knits. They are also one of the most versatile belts, as you can wear them just below the bust line, on the waist, on the hips or through belt loops on trousers or skirts.

The wide belt
This belt will add drama to almost any outfit. Opt for one that's as wide as your waist allows, and wear it over chunky knits or even over coats, as Kate does, to cinch in heavy fabrics and keep your silhouette feminine. A wide belt can accentuate your waist, enhance curves and cleverly conceal any lumps and bumps.

The textured belt
Add contrast and interest to plain fabrics with a textured or shiny belt, such as Kate's mock-croc "Betony" seen here.

The statement colour belt
To brighten up a Little Black Dress or to add subtle, elegant detail to colourful outfits, pick a belt in a bright colour. The belt can either tone with or contrast with other pieces in your outfit – it's up to you. Kate often pairs a chunky red belt from Reiss with a matching red coat.

The elasticated belt
Worn on the waist, this tight-fitting belt will give you curves, even if you don't already have them (and helps control them if you do), creating a classic hourglass effect. For a different look, you can also wear an elasticated belt lower down on your hips.

The Earrings Kate's earrings are very similar in design to her heavily favoured citrine and diamond Kiki McDonough earrings, which are thought to have been a Christmas present from William. Fashion observers suspect that the Duchess loved the first pair so much that she commissioned McDonough to create her an additional pair using different coloured stones.

Kate's Bespoke LBD

The Dress Kate once more took the gold medal for style when she wore this beautiful dress to attend a reception for Great Britain's Olympic medalists, hosted by HM the Queen at Buckingham Palace on October 23, 2012. The champion athletes in attendance wore their official Olympic black suits adorned with their gold medals, and Kate carefully selected an outfit in a matching colour palette.

The Duchess chose a black dress embellished with lace and gold flowers, designed by one of her go-to designers, Alice Temperley. The piece was made for the Duchess personally, frustrating fans who were knocked out by this twist on that favourite style stand-by: the Little Black Dress. Fashion writers thought the starting point for the dress was the "Esmeralda" from Temperley London's collection, as the lace detailing, belled sleeves and ruffled hems were similar in style and shape to this off-the-rack piece. However, added to this simple base was gold, ivory and dusky rose floral embroidery, sheer detailing over the décolletage and a signature Kate staple: a waist belt in the form of a soft, satin bow.

Alice Temperley has spoken about how it feels to be a favourite designer of both Middleton sisters: "I'm flattered," she said. "They're the most humble, down-to-earth people I've ever dressed. They're completely easy and wonderful to work with, and they look great in the clothes. They know exactly what they like. When I was dressing them, I had no idea what a reaction the world would have," she added. "I hope that they always get the support that they deserve because they are truly good girls."

The Shoes On her feet, the Duchess wore her Jimmy Choo "Cosmic" pumps, which take the form of a classic court shoe but are stylistically notched up a level with the addition of a platform under the toes, giving the traditional look a more modern profile.

The Bracelet Kate wore her diamond flower cluster Art Deco bracelet to the royal reception. One of her favourite pieces of jewellery, it often graces her wrist on dressier occasions. It is thought to have been a gift from William, possibly once belonging to his mother, Princess Diana.

Customize like Kate

Kate's Temperley dress had embroidery and a fitted lace panel to make it unique for her. Even if you're not on a personal-name basis with designers, you, too, can create a one-of-a-kind piece with a little savvy sewing ...

Embellish away
If you're a dab hand with a needle and thread, purchase some cheap netting and get creative. However, if you're less artistically inclined, most haberdashers stock a selection of embroidered fabrics. Simply choose one you think will work and stitch the fabric panels onto sleeves and hemlines of a plain dress to add a touch of drama.

Belt up
With nothing more than a length of satin ribbon, you can add waist detailing (one of Kate's key fashion rules) to any outfit. Simply wrap a length of ribbon around your waistline and fasten with a neat bow.

Make a feature of modesty
By adding a sheer panel to the plunging neckline of her dress, Kate transformed this piece into a suitably demure dress for a Duchess attending a royal reception. You can do the same by simply purchasing a piece of sheer netting or lace in the same colour as your dress and stitching it in place over the neckline and or arms.

Button up
An easy way to add a touch of your own personal style to a high-street piece is to replace the buttons. Haberdashers are full of interesting and unusual buttons, so scout around for some truly unique options.

Add a dash of contrasting fabric
Update plain polo necks or cardigans by sewing a band of tweed or leather (perhaps salvaged from old unworn clothes) just above the bustline or onto the waist. You can also try sewing elbow patches to a sweater or blazer. This simple patch-up job adds instant designer detailing and flair to tired pieces.

FAR LEFT: Kate wore this striking cream chiffon Temperley frock, with black detailing at the cuffs, collar and waist, for her first public appearance after her engagement announcement, when attending the Teenage Cancer Trust Christmas Spectacular in Norfolk in December 2010.

LEFT: The Duchess looks a true Queen of the South Pacific with her "crown" of flower garlands and the floral Alice by Temperley "Beatrice" dress she wore on the Polynesian island Tuvalu, during her South Pacific tour in September 2012.

RIGHT: While watching the tennis at Wimbledon in June 2011, Kate stood out from the crowd in this on-theme white ruffled and pleated Temperley "Moriah" dress.

Kate's Sheer Beauty

The Dress Fashion and St Andrews University have always played a big part in Kate's life. It was during a St Andrews charity fashion event at a catwalk show in March 2002 that Kate first caught the eye of her fellow student, Prince William. After seeing his future wife modelling a mostly see-through dress (see page 22), the Prince apparently whispered to a friend: "Wow, Kate's hot!" This sheer dress, made from black and turquoise knitted silk by Charlotte Todd, fashion graduate of the University of the West of England, was sold at auction in 2011 for a staggering £65,000 ($105,300)!

To show her support for her alma mater (and that of her patron husband, too), when the royal couple attended the 600th anniversary gala on November 8, 2012, Kate cheekily chose another sheer dress … although this time something much more sophisticated, from one of her favourite designers, Alice Temperley.

The show-stopping "Amoret" gown is made of luxurious French lace underlaid with a blush silk slip that accentuates the floral. Typical Temperley detailing can also be found in the scalloping along the cuffs, hem and the plunging neckline, a keyhole back, crepe bow belt and a curved seam, which lends elegant movement to the skirt. The overall effect is a supremely feminine, timeless dress that is the ultimate in refined chic and evening glamour.

The gorgeous floor-length gown was, in fact, first seen on Kate at the premiere of Steven Spielberg's *War Horse* in January 2012 in Leicester Square, London. However, this time the effect was slightly different. Never one to miss a fashion reference, Kate must have been aware that the sheer nature of this lace dress would recall the earlier, somewhat infamous, see-through dress of her student days. How typically clever of Kate to turn what is actually a demure dress into a rather racy inside fashion joke. Indeed, that fateful day was clearly on Kate's mind at the gala as she joked with a current female undergraduate at St Andrews University: "I hope you weren't involved in the fashion show – you never know what you are going to be asked to wear!"

The Shoes The Duchess also brought back her towering black suede Jimmy Choo "Cosmic" heels. The teetering platforms balanced the length of the gown and added extra height and drama to Kate's already statuesque frame.

The Brooch This gala event came just three days before Remembrance Day on November 11, 2012 – a period when many people wear a red poppy in memory of those who sacrificed their lives during active duty. A staunch supporter of the Armed Forces (with husband Prince William an active member of the Royal Air Force), Kate pinned a large poppy-shaped brooch, plated with 18-carat gold and inlaid with red and black crystals, to her dress. All profits raised from the sale of this Adrian Buckley-designed piece went to the Royal British Legion, a leading charity that supports serving and ex-Service personnel in the British Armed Forces. British designer Buckley founded his eponymous line in 1989 and has since won the prestigious award for Best Costume Jewellery four times at the UK Jewellery Awards.

The Bag Kate picked up on the poppy colour in her ruby-red Alexander McQueen "Classic" clutch, albeit without the signature McQueen skull clasp. In its place at the centre of the bowed bag was a bespoke clasp, embellished with three red rhinestones. This was another recycled piece – Kate having first carried it on the Thames Diamond Jubilee River Pageant, back in June 2012.

OPPOSITE: The simple Annoushka "Baroque Pearl Drop" earrings, top left, are one of Kate's favourites, as their classic, understated design works equally well with day- and eveningwear. Kate has been spotted wearing the beautiful diamond bracelet and matching diamond drop earrings, right and bottom right, to many formal evening functions. This set was first seen on Kate's tour of Canada in 2011, but a designer has never been identified, and they are described only as being "a gift". This has led to speculation that the set may have been a bespoke design, specially created as a present for her by Prince William.

Wear Sheer Fabrics with Class

Tracing Kate's love for sheer fabrics is a key way to see how her youthful experimentation has evolved into a mature style. Worn carefully, sheer fabric can be the epitome of sophistication and – unlike *that* runway dress – Kate has now mastered the art of demure when it comes to the transparent. Here are some of her style tricks …

Slip into something a little special
A nude slip will keep a sheer outfit classy, not crass, and also skim over any lumps and bumps – not that Kate has any to hide!

Play with patterns
Patterned sheer fabrics, such as lace, provide more coverage than the sheer netting in which young Kate once strutted down the catwalk.

Foxy folds
Another of Kate's style staples – the pleated skirt – works very well in sheer fabrics, such as chiffon, as the folds create layers, which prevent it from being too revealing.

Master the covered/uncovered look
A dress in a sheer fabric with long, bell-shaped sleeves and a full skirt is fast becoming a staple of Kate's wardrobe. The hint of flesh through the fabric adds glamour but the delicate sheer covering keeps things elegant.

Fabulous Retro Chic

The Dress Kate wore this exquisite emerald-green Mulberry dress to the opening of the "Treasures" exhibition at the Natural History Museum in London on November 27, 2012. The "Full Pleated Shirt Dress" from Mulberry's ready-to-wear collection features a Peter Pan collar, a plethora of pleats, a belted waist and long balloon sleeves gathered at the cuff. The 100 per cent silk dress has retro styling, including Mulberry's "Peace and Love" jacquard design, and the rich colour is given the somewhat unglamorous official name of "cabbage"!

It is not the first time that Kate has been associated with classic British design house Mulberry. She took their "Polly Push" bag in midnight blue on her tour of Canada and has been spotted in a wool skirt by the brand while shopping on the King's Road in Chelsea. In fact, the exhibition was not the first time Kate has worn this particular piece. One year previously, almost to the day, she first wore what is, for the Duchess, an uncharacteristically "boho-styled" retro frock, while launching the Queen's Diamond Jubilee celebrations at Buckingham Palace.

Mulberry is well known for its quintessentially English style, so this more flamboyant dress was out of the ordinary not only for the Duchess, but also for the label itself. The company describes the dress as "prim and proper with a Mulberry twist. The full-pleated shirt dress will not let you blend into the crowd." Perhaps Kate felt safe experimenting with a brand like Mulberry, which has a solid reputation for classic style – here, she can play with a quirky look without fear of going too far.

The Shoes Kate once more stepped into her favourite Jimmy Choo "Cosmic" pumps – this time the matt suede fabric of the heels perfectly offset her shimmering silk dress.

The Hair Kate may have been wearing an old dress and shoes to a museum, but she did wear one brand new item that caused worldwide excitement: her hairstyle. Perhaps influenced by the boho dress, the Duchess chose a retro look that featured a parted side fringe and flicky layers. The overall effect was not dissimilar to the famous style of 1970s star Farrah Fawcett – or indeed, as many observers were quick to point out – some of the hairstyles sported by Princess Diana in the early 1980s. Kate's new look is thought to have been created by her favourite hair salon – Richard Ward of Chelsea, London – and was widely deemed to be a great success, softening her face and adding sophistication.

Flick It like Kate

The Duchess's 1970s-inspired hairstyle is, in fact, pretty easy to achieve if you follow a few simple steps …

Embrace your dark side
Kate took her natural colour up a shade from soft, light-tinged auburn tones to a sleeker, richer, chocolate-brown. Going for a slightly darker shade than your natural hair colour will help create a fuller, sleeker look.

Fringe benefits
Ask your hairdresser to cut the front section of your hair into a long fringe at a steep angle because a straight, blunt cut can look too severe. Make sure it's left long enough to tuck behind the ears in case you have a change of heart!

Layer up
Ask your stylist for additional layers to be chopped into the lower lengths around your face to add texture, volume and movement.

Big on body
When washing your hair, be sure to rinse out all traces of conditioner to prevent your hair from going limp. Then, while it's still wet, use a volumizing spray at the roots before you begin blow-drying.

Get to grips with your hairdryer
Rough-dry your hair until it's about 90 per cent dry, teasing it with your fingertips to encourage volume. Then, starting at the bottom, take 2.5–5 cm (1–2 in) sections at a time, keeping the rest of your hair pinned out of the way. Wrap each section around a large, round, bristle brush, lift the hair up with maximum tension and direct the dryer onto it for a few seconds. Use the cool setting on your dryer to fix each section before removing the brush, and then mist with a flexible light-hold hairspray.

Finally, get to work on your fringe
If it has already dried, spritz your fringe with a little cold water. Then, using a smaller, round brush, start drying with a rolling action. As the hair becomes drier, begin brushing the fringe at the desired angle to create a flick.

Finishing touches
In order for the curl to really last, put in some large Velcro curlers and leave for 10 minutes, blasting them with a hot hairdryer. Remove the rollers when your hair is cool, and use your fingertips to tease out the curls. Again, finish off with a spritz of hairspray.

Learn from the professionals
Kate's favourite Richard Ward salon is just one of many hairdressers that now offer blow-drying master classes, so you can learn how to create a professional finish in the comfort of your own home.

LOOK 39

Tartan Celebration

The Coat Kate made a savvy style statement when she visited her old preparatory school, St Andrew's in Pangbourne, Berkshire, on November 30, 2012. Her bespoke Alexander McQueen coat was made out of Black Watch tartan, which was both an appropriate choice for a visit that took place on St Andrew's Day, and a clever reference to Kate's old school uniform. The three-check pattern featuring blue and green separated by black was very similar to the kilts worn by Kate as a pupil at the fee-paying private school between 1986 and 1995. But the coat wasn't just an exercise in nostalgia – Kate was also picking up on a very current fashion trend, with tartan a key look on many autumn/winter 2012 catwalks, including Chloe, Michael Kors and Ralph Lauren, as well as McQueen.

For McQueen's Autumn 2012 collections, Sarah Burton selected the very striking Black Watch tartan, belonging to Scotland's most famous elite army regiment, which dates back as far as 1729. At the time, the brand released the following statement about its fabric choice: "The use of the navy and dark-green plaid of Scotland's 3rd Battalion Regiment, the Black Watch, represents the brand's reverence for history and tradition."

Kate's coat-dress was, in fact, custom-made, but it incorporates some elements of the Alexander McQueen "Black Watch" coat, from the label's hipper and more affordable diffusion range, McQ. Both the full skirt and oversized flaps at the hips reflect the original design. However, Kate's coat was cut from a lighter weight of the fabric, making it a little easier to wear.

The Boots Once again, Kate donned her favourite black Aquatalia "Rhumba" boots, pulling them over thick black tights. And, once again, the versatile and practical boots didn't let her down on the sports field. Seemingly delighted to be back on familiar turf, the former team captain showed off her skills on the school's new hockey pitch, looking totally at ease – even in high heels!

The Earrings Kate picked out the navy in her coat-dress in her dazzling sapphire and diamond earrings. This reworked pair of her late mother-in-law Diana's earrings is clearly a favourite with the Duchess, as she has worn them on many occasions (see also Look 6, page 42). The heirloom jewellery also helped underline the shades of Diana that many observers saw in her still-new, side-swept hairstyle.

Tart Up Tartan

The Duchess of Cambridge has a fondness for this traditional checked fabric, and twice carried a folded Strathearn tartan scarf in a nod to her Scottish title, the Countess of Strathearn. The first time she sported the scarf was with her scarlet Alexander McQueen outfit for the Thames Diamond Jubilee Pageant in London on June 2012 (see Look 22, page 96) and then again in July in Edinburgh, when she watched Prince William honoured with the highest possible title in Scotland: the Knight of the Thistle.

On this occasion, Kate's tartan coat may have matched the student uniforms of her old prep school, but there was nothing of the schoolgirl about this sophisticated outfit. Here are some dos and don'ts for wearing this traditional Scottish fabric in a stylish, grown-up way …

Do remember it's a winter fabric
Tartan is too heavy for summer but you can still keep the thick fabric looking feminine by choosing pieces in well-tailored shapes.

Don't overdo it
One piece of tartan is always enough, as Kate knows well. Wear tartan alone as the main feature item in any outfit, as the pattern looks stunning in a solid block, but the effect will be lost when worn on top of matching tartan accessories. Similarly, a touch of tartan – in the form of a scarf or handbag – adds another dimension to an otherwise plain outfit.

Do wear it for all occasions
Tartan is a versatile fabric that can be dressed up or down. Add simple black accessories and heels for formal events, or combine with denim and long boots for more casual daywear.

Don't forget tartan was originally worn by men
To soften its masculine look, try choosing feminine shapes such as Kate's full-skirted "fit and flare" coat.

Do choose the size of your tartan plaid with care
This is not the kind of fabric where bigger is better for most women – both petite and larger frames will find finer checks more flattering than bold, large designs.

OPPOSITE: Despite Kate's fresh-faced appearance, just three days after she wore this stylish tartan ensemble to visit her old school, it was announced that the Duchess was pregnant and had been suffering from a severe form of morning sickness. This led to Kate spending a few days in hospital, but Buckingham Palace soon assured the nation that Kate and the baby, due in July 2013, were in good health.

Kate's Blooming

The Dress When the Duchess of Cambridge attended
the unveiling of her portrait at the National Portrait Gallery
on January 12, 2013, she was glowing with health, and her
slender frame hinted at the first signs of a still-tiny baby
bump. The mother-to-be displayed a rosy complexion with
pink cheeks, and despite looking her usual slim self, she did
appear a little fuller in the face. One thing seemed clear –
the Duchess appeared to be back on form following her brief
hospitalization with severe morning sickness.

Despite any distraction caused by her pregnancy, Kate's
impeccable sense of style shone through as she donned
this elegant burgundy chiffon frock for an event that would
inevitably put her under the spotlight. The "Sofie Rae"
dress was from her high-street favourite, Whistles, and was
actually part of their Autumn/Winter 2011 collection. The
seasonal design is 100 per cent silk, with long, floaty sleeves,
a deep V-neckline and open-neck with collarless trim. Its full,
pleated skirt falls flatteringly to just-below-knee length and
gathers at the waist for definition. Kate chose to add her own
plain wide ribbon-style black belt to pull the look together,
matching with her black shoes and clutch bag.

Not yet ready for maternity wear and always keen to get
maximum use out of a purchase, the Duchess was previously
spotted wearing this dress when she and Prince William
travelled to Denmark back in November 2011 for the charity
UNICEF, and she also wore it under a plum wool coat by an
independent British designer, when she visited Newcastle in
October 2012.

While Kate's fashion sense was typically faultess, the
official portrait of her, by British-born artist Paul Emsley,
inspired more mixed reviews, as many commentators
thought the likeness unflattering. Some critics felt the
painting made the Duchess look old, while the *Daily Mail*
reported that the portrait had been called "rotten". The
Duchess herself, however, said she was thrilled with the
results, and husband Prince William also had high praise for
the painting, stating: "It's beautiful, it's absolutely beautiful."
To pose for the portrait, Kate wore a navy pussy-bow
sleeveless, silk blouse by French Connection, called the "Sub
Silky Tie Top", and accessorized with the sapphire and
diamond earrings that were refashioned from a set belonging
to Princess Diana.

The Necklace To complement the "Sofie Rae" dress, Kate chose to wear her much-loved Asprey 167 Button Pendant, which nestled perfectly in the frock's deep V-neck. The necklace features white pavé diamonds surrounding a central amethyst, all set in 18-carat white gold. Demand for the item since Kate was first seen wearing it in 2011 was so high that jewellers Asprey decided to re-issue the previously discontinued piece in September 2012. Asprey is one of the UK's oldest, fine jewellery shops, dating back to 1781, with a flagship store on London's New Bond Street. Asprey has a long association with royalty, supplying crowns, coronets and sceptres for royal families around the world, and it currently holds a Royal Warrant of appointment from The Prince of Wales.

The Shoes The early stages of pregnancy didn't seem to affect Kate's penchant for high heels. Here she wears another previously seen pair, her Episode "Angel" shoes in black suede. The Episode brand is sold only in House of Fraser department stores. Kate was first spotted wearing these heels during the Diamond Jubilee visit to Leicester in March 2012.

How to Dress your Bump

Kate's pregnancy remains unchanged – chic, elegant, ladylike shapes and a seamless blend of high-street and designer labels. Many first-time mothers-to-be make the mistake of ditching their favourite clothes too early, but Kate understands that just because you have a bump to dress, it doesn't mean you have to lose your sense of style. Here's how to look good in clothes that have room for a good-sized bump but still show off your figure and style credentials ...

Be beautifully wrapped
Wrap-around dresses and tops make a great choice for mums-to-be, as the V-neck front flatters the chest, while the tied waist allows for the growth of the bump. Wrap-arounds work for both day and evening, and the springy jersey fabric allows you to get away with your normal size for the first six months of pregnancy.

Be biased
Kate loves dresses and skirts cut on the bias, and the soft-draping, curve-accentuating lines are perfect for pregnancy, as they have more "give" than straight-cut ones and will sit well on your bump as it gets bigger.

Find full-term friends in your wardrobe
There will probably be a few things in your wardrobe that you can wear throughout your pregnancy with a little bit of alteration. For example, cardigans and shirts can be worn open with a long camisole top underneath.

Say no to frills and fuss
As you will be carrying plenty of bulk on your top half, don't add to it with overly fussy tops. Keep detail to a minimum.

Show off your shape
Define your figure by choosing long tops with ties that do up under the bust or at the side. For more glamorous evening events, add thick ribbon or belts to shapeless tops and dresses.

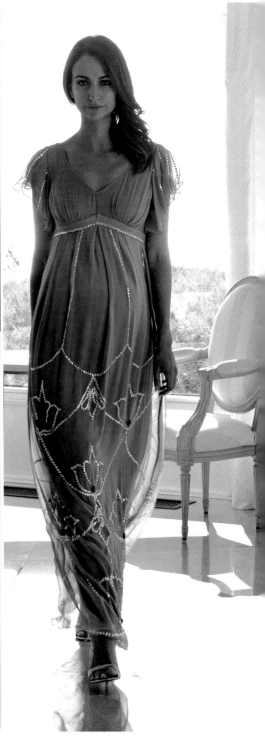

Mums the Word!

Thankfully Kate is spoilt for choice when it comes to maternity wear, as these days shops and fashion designers have finally realized that women want to remain looking chic and not hide their bumps in shapeless smocks for nine months. Here are some of the best places to shop for Kate-style elegant maternity fashion …

ASOS Maternity Collection, *www.asos.com*
Rumour has it Kate stocked up on some pretty items from this online shop's own-brand maternity line, which features fashion-forward dresses, jeans and lingerie.

Gap, *www.gap.com*
In January 2013 Kate was spotted browsing the Chelsea, London, branch of Gap, everybody's favourite go-to for comfy but well-cut casuals. And no wonder – they do a fantastic range of maternity jeans, which have the same cut as their standard denims, but with an added elastic extending waistline that grows with your bump.

Isabella Oliver, *www.isabellaoliver.com*
This classy online store has become the saviour of many style-conscious mums-to-be who love their flattering runched jersey tops and fabulous range of wrap dresses, which promise to add glamour to any bump.

Séraphine, *www.seraphine.com*
A great choice for chic maternity clothes that flaunt, rather than hide, your curves, Séraphine would be perfect for Kate as many of their colours and shapes closely echo Kate's signature style: as their purple knot dress (top left), stone wool frock coat (bottom left) and grey chiffon and sequin dress (opposite) demonstrate.

Top Shop Maternity, *www.topshop.com*
The Duchess has always been a fan of this store's affordable but on-trend offerings, so it makes perfect sense for her to choose from their great range of trendy mum-to-be essential wear.

Proud in Polka Dots

The Dress In April 2013 Kate may have been almost seven months pregnant with Prince George, but she still managed to reinforce her accessible style credentials by looking fantastic in a black and white polka dot dress – from British high street store Topshop.

The Duke and Duchess of Cambridge and Prince Harry were on an official engagement to open the £100 million Harry Potter attraction at the Warner Bros Studios in Hertfordshire.

The royals were joined by Harry Potter author J.K. Rowling for the grand opening – and the world's most famous writer also happened to be wearing a polka dot dress.

Kate's spotty dress – named "The Florence" – was at the time a very popular Topshop style, available in various prints and colourways. The many styles of Florence did include maternity versions, however despite being in her third trimester of pregnancy, it seems as if Kate was wearing a non-maternity version – highlighting just how neat and tidy her advanced bump had remained.

Naturally, the "Kate effect" struck again as her dotty look inspired mums-to-be everywhere and the Topshop dress quickly sold out. In fact, the Topshop website was listing The Florence as "out of stock" within just one hour of the Duchess of Cambridge being pictured in it!

The Jacket Kate teamed the high street dress with an old favourite – her black ruffle-trim Ralph Lauren jacket. The Duchess loves to match this simple staple with a host of outfits, and has been photographed in it many times – perhaps most notably the day after her wedding to Prince William, when she teamed it with a pretty blue Zara dress for her "going away" outfit.

The Shoes and Bag Showing you can still get away with mid-heeled shoes while pregnant, Kate added glamour to the dress with her black Episode "Angel" pumps from House of Fraser. The suede shoes feature a slim platform sole, which is better balanced and easier to walk in while pregnant than a typical thin shoe sole, as it distributes the extra weight more evenly. A long-term style standby, these shoes first made their debut when Kate wore them with her Issa blue dress to officially announce her engagement. She has worn them time and again since, often teamed, as here, with a simple black suede clutch purse.

The Earrings Not for the first time, Kate finishes off this simple day outfit with her Annoushka pearl drop earrings – designed by the British jeweller and founder of the famous

Links of London, Annoushka Ducas. This particular style is known as the "Classic Baroque Drop". The earrings retail at around £310 ($405) and are made from creamy white freshwater pearls, selected for their even shape and warm lustre, hung on 18-carat gold rings.

Copy Kate's Maternity Style

Despite struggling with acute morning sickness during the early months of all her pregnancies and needing bed rest, the Duchess has remained a picture of chic composure whenever in the public eye. She knows what works for her, choosing clothes for their comfort and clean lines – often shunning specific "maternity" wear for looser, more flowing shapes from the non-maternity labels she loves. Here are some of Kate's clever pregnancy style tricks ...

Stay streamlined with a tailored coat
One of Kate's favourite garments to wear while pregnant is a fitted coat, as this covers and protects her bump while still looking streamlined. Her usual choice is a block, often bold colour, with a buttoned-down front. Wearing a structured coat over your outfit instantly makes you feel put together and chic. This doesn't have to be a specific maternity item, simply pick one that is more tailored at the shoulders and arms but with a slight A-line silhouette that will accommodate your growing belly.

Trim down with a tunic
Another favourite maternity look of Kate's is a tunic dress or top. Comfortable and flattering, this shape nips in under the bust rather than around the waist, making it a perfect way to show off the trimmer top third of your body, while gently skimming your bump.

Pick a print
The Duchess is a fan of prints in general, and this doesn't stop when she is pregnant. Be it polka dots, animal prints, tartan or floral, she often decorates her bump with a pretty pattern – dispelling the myth that you should avoid bold prints while pregnant. In fact, for Kate, the right print just enhances her growing bump.

Dare to bare those legs
Part of Kate's normal demure look is to favour skirts that fall just below the knee, but to avoid looking frumpy as her body shape changes during pregnancy, Kate often raises her usual hemline a few inches – as with the Topshop dress seen opposite. By opting for a just-above-the-knee length she manages to draw the eye to her still-slender legs while remaining elegant.

Don't ditch your heels
Many pregnant woman switch to flats but Kate shows you don't have to if you choose carefully – just be sure they have a platform sole for hidden extra support, easy balance and less backache. Luckily for Kate, her all-time favourite wedge shape fits the bill perfectly.

LOOK 42

A Stylish Introduction

The Dress As Kate came down the steps of the Lindo maternity wing of St Mary's Hospital, London at 7.15 p.m. on July 22, 2013, she knew she would be met by an even bigger crowd of well-wishers and photographers than normal. Thousands had gathered to get a first glimpse of the small bundle of joy cradled in her arms – Kate and William's first child, Prince George.

Even after a tiring nine-hour labour during which the summer temperature outside soared to more than 104 degrees, the Duchess didn't disappoint her fans, looking every inch the glowing yet groomed new mother.

When it came to selecting a dress for an occasion that was destined for the front pages of newspapers across the globe, Kate looked no further than Jenny Packham – one of her all-time favourite designers. Indeed, the legendary British designer has provided the Duchess with dresses for many of her most important public outings over the last six years.

For this joyful moment, Kate opted for a cornflower blue empire-line dress with ivory spots, custom-made by Packham just for her.

Many onlookers noted a poignant tribute to Diana, Princess of Wales, in this choice of dress, as her late mother-in-law had also selected polka dots when she stood on the exact same steps at St Mary's, some 31 years ago while holding the newborn Prince William.

The flattering dress skimmed gently over Kate's still rounded belly and coordinated perfectly with both her trusty pale wedges and the ivory blanket swaddling young Prince George.

The Hair and Make-up With artfully tousled hair and a glowing complexion, the Duchess of Cambridge introduced George to the world in trademark glossy style. Despite the long labour, she looked as fresh as if she had just returned from a gentle summer stroll.

Behind the just-stepped-from-the-salon effect was the Duchess's personal hairdresser, Amanda Cook Tucker, who also cuts the hair of Princes William and Harry. Cook Tucker often accompanies the Duchess on foreign tours, including her Diamond Jubilee tour to the Far East in September 2012. Here, Kate's shiny locks looked longer than ever, smoothed out and then gently teased into soft maternal waves at the ends.

Although the Duchess does use other hairstylists, with Richard Ward another favourite, she is thought to regard Mrs Cook Tucker as a trusted insider – exactly the kind of reliable friend you call whenever you're feeling the most pressure.

As for Kate's new mum make-up glow – a barely-there look consisting of coral lipstick, soft brown eyeshadow, eyeliner and pretty pink blusher – it seems most likely it was applied by the Duchess herself, who generally prefers to do her own make-up.

How to Glow in Your Post-Delivery Pics

Of course, the single most important part of the post-birth experience is holding a healthy, happy baby in your arms. But there's also no harm in wanting to look your best for those all-important first photos – after all, they will be framed, put on social media and seen by pretty much everyone you know. Here are a few easy tricks to ensure you look great for that special moment.

Get a blow-dry
Have a trim and blow-dry close to your due date, and if you're having a planned C-section, you can even have your hair done that morning. Don't think of it as being vain – it'll be harder to find time for such pampering with a newborn, so take the opportunity to spoil yourself now.

Have natural make-up handy
Pack a pared-down purse of make-up essentials in your hospital bag. It's best to keep it simple, but don't feel like you should go completely bare-faced either. The trick is to look natural – but with a little help from staples such as foundation, concealer, blusher, lip gloss and mascara. This kit will go a long way when you're fighting against unflattering hospital lighting and lack of sleep!

Pre-plan your hospital outfit
Instead of being snapped in one of those standard-issue hospital gowns, pack a pretty nightdress and dressing gown to change into for photos. Bright colours will help counter the hospital backdrop.

LOOK 43

Kate: Still a High-Street Hero

The Dress On February 14, 2014, some seven months after the birth of Prince George, Kate grabbed our attention in a sharply-tailored electric blue dress, made by high street retailer L.K. Bennet. The occasion was one of her first official solo engagements – a school visit in west London, where she opened new facilities on behalf of The Art Room. This enterprising charity helps young people with mental health issues, a subject close to the hearts of both Kate and William.

Showing no sign of sleepless nights, the Duchess flaunted her enviably trim post-baby figure in the slim-fitting "Detroit" dress by the London brand perhaps more famous for its shoes. Despite visiting the school on St Valentine's Day, Kate shied away from more obvious reds and pinks, and plumped for a brilliant, vibrant blue hue. The colour is described by L.K. Bennett as "snorkel blue" and featured heavily in their Spring/Summer 2014 collection.

The dress, which is beautifully crafted with expertly placed panels and a cinched waist, created a flattering hourglass shape on Kate, with the bold shade exuding fashion confidence. All told, it was another classic example of Kate's effortless style at affordable prices.

Made from polyester crepe fabric, the dress also features three-quarter length sleeves and a "notch collar" detail neckline. Most seasons L.K. Bennett release a dress that is similar in style to the Detroit, but they distinguish it from year to year with new tailoring details or different colours. What remains constant is the flattering, fitted cut, a skirt that hits just below the knee and sharp details at the bust.

As many fashion fans will know, the top-end high street store L.K. Bennett is one of Kate's go-to brands, primarily for shoes and daywear. Indeed, the Duchess loved this look so much she wore the £225 ($295) dress again, in August of the same year, to visit the poppy remembrance installation with Prince William at The Tower of London. Here, the bright blue colour contrasted with the sea of ceramic red poppies, created to honour the thousands of servicemen who lost their lives during the First World War. On both occasions, Kate set off the striking dress with a simple dark clutch bag and pumps, natural make-up and long, wavy hair.

The Jewellery Eagle-eyed Kate followers were quick to spot that on Valentine's Day the Duchess sported an apparently brand new watch from classic French designer, Cartier – the £5,500 ($7,210) Ballon Bleu in stainless steel. Described by the design house as: "Floating like a balloon and as blue as the sapphire safely nestled in its side, it adds a dash of elegance to male and female wrists alike."

Also being debuted on this day was a new pair of earrings from another much-loved jewellery designer – Kiki McDonough. This time Kate opted for her green amethyst and diamond cushion-drop earrings, priced at £1,200 ($1,575).

Completing the look was a favourite necklace – a Mappin & Webb Fortune White Gold Drop Pendant necklace, featuring 0.67 carats of round brilliant-set diamonds in three 18-carat white gold infinity loops. This beautiful piece, said to symbolize luck and good fortune, retails for around £3,950 ($5,180), and again is teamed with a simple black suede clutch purse.

OPPOSITE: True blue: Kate wows in an eye-catching cornflower Alexander McQueen belted coat-dress, while marking the 70th anniversary of D-Day in France, 2014.

Be Bold with Bright Blue

While the Duchess of Cambridge has experimented with wearing a full rainbow of colours over the years, she routinely comes back to the vivid blue end of the spectrum – from crisp colbolts to proud periwinkles.

Blue seems to be Kate's "happy shade" – the colour that makes her feel confident and on top form – whether she's stepping out for an official engagement, walking the red carpet, or simply out shopping. She has worked this one colour in countless different ways – and so can you. Brilliant blues suit most skin tones, are easy to combine with other colours and can complement any occasion, from the formal to informal. Here are some tips on being bold with blue …

Team it with black
Electric blue works fabulously mixed with black to create a strong and striking look. Choose this colour pair for evening events, adding black shoes and classic pearl or gold jewellery for a touch of vintage glamour.

Mellow with yellow
For a more relaxed look, try mixing bright blue with a mustard top, or ochre handbag and shoes. Bear in mind the lighter the yellow shade, the softer the look, but why not experiment with canary yellow for a take-no-prisoners unrestrained style statement?

Wear with whites
If you have a formal occasion you want to impress at, mix bold blue with white for a dignified, regal look. Lace or metallic accessories will add a modern edge to this strong shade.

Neutralize the effect
In order to soften up this powerful shade of blue, you can use neutral colours such as tan or beige. For example, a nude dress under an electric blue blazer. This creates a great day look that is casual, yet elegant at the same time.

Handsome in Houndstooth

The Dress By October 2015 Kate was back in front of the cameras for her first official engagement since giving birth to her second child, Princess Charlotte, five months earlier. Sporting a noteworthy fringe, Kate chose a striking black and white Ralph Lauren houndstooth belted dress for her visit to the Anna Freud Centre in north London. Kate was officially there to lend her support to a centre that works with children with mental health problems, but for style watchers who had been hotly awaiting her return, the Duchess certainly didn't disappoint.

Back in the spotlight once more, Kate was channelling pure Parisian chic in the £1,200 ($1,575) "Austin" silk dress from Ralph Lauren's Black Label – a garment the fashion house accurately describes as "the quintessential shirtdress". The black and white frock was cinched at the waist with a thin black belt, which happened to perfectly showcase how Kate's middle had returned to its former tiny shape following baby number two. With distinctive barrel cuffs on the long sleeves and a skirt that flares out at the hem for a flirty, flattering finish, the grown-up dress shape could be said to represent a subtle style evolution for the demure Duchess.

The Hair To complete her well-tailored comeback, Kate was showing off her new flicked hairstyle, complete with a fringe. This was the first time we'd seen the Duchess with a long fringe since November 2012. The new "do" was created for her once again by another of her most trusted hairdressers, Chelsea-based Richard Ward. Ward is someone Kate has turned to on numerous occasions in the past for his particular skill at transforming her brunette locks into flawless bouncing curls.

Unsurprisingly, the new style caused waves and shortly afterwards Richard Ward was interviewed on British talk show *This Morning,* where he coined the term "gringe" to describe the kind of "grown-out fringe" he had given Kate.

"A longer, sweeping fringe is a great way to experiment without the risk factor of a complete restyle," he told *This Morning*. "These kind of fringes suit most people as they're extremely soft and feminine and they work well whether you have long or short hair. They aren't too bold but can completely change your look without having to lose any length, and are easy to grow out if you're not quite sure. They're timeless and ageless – they never really go out of fashion."

The Shoes and Bag The dress shape and hair may have been something of a departure for Kate, but the Duchess stuck to trusted favourites when it came to accessories. She paired the handsome printed frock with her much-worn Spanish-made £260 ($340) Stuart Weitzman black "Power" pumps, along with her black £495 ($650) Mulberry "Bayswater" clutch – a purse she also owns in two other colours – cream and brown.

Making Monochrome Magic

As Kate demonstrates here – and not for the first time – you can't go wrong with a classic monochrome print. Black and white is probably the easiest colour combination to pull off, with nearly any clothing mix guaranteed to look crisp, modern and effortlessly chic. Here's how to make monochrome work for you …

Wear it top-to-toe
Monochrome is at its most effective and striking when worn from head-to-toe, including matching accessories. Try teaming a black and white dress with black shoes and handbag to get started. But watch out for a white top and black skirt as you can easily look more waitress than princess.

Pick a print
As Kate's houndtooth Ralph Lauren shirtdress shows, print can help break up the starkness of black and white on its own. Prints can also make the monochrome look a little softer – creating a more understated, demure aesthetic.

Work it out
Black and white striped shirts work well when worn with tapered trousers and a longline jacket, just add black heels to finish off a strong work outfit. A black and white tweed suit, teamed with a black shirt, meanwhile will also look fresh but office smart.

Vintage glamour
There's a reason why film stars of the 1940s and 50s continued to dress in black and white print dresses long after the advent of colour films. The black and white contrast simply exudes timeless glamour and sophistication. Team with a bold red lipstick to channel pure screen siren.

Look for stripes of piping
Black trousers with a stripe of white going all the way down the side are a great way to build monochrome into a look without overdoing it. Just pair with a black top to keep the overall look streamlined.

Add a splash of colour
Yes, we all know monochrome means black and white, but surely rules are there to be broken from time to time? So if you are wary of removing all colour from your outfit, break up the monochrome print by adding a pop of colour, such as a neon scarf, a bright-coloured handbag or jacket.

LOOK 45

Bold and Beautiful in Blooms

The Dress Kate showed the world just how fashion fearless she had become on October 27, 2015, when she wore this dramatic multicoloured evening gown by designer Erdem to attend a black-tie dinner.

As a patron of the 100 Women in Hedge Funds' Philanthropic Initiatives, the Duchess was at the annual Hedge Fund Gala event to present the European Leadership Award.

Kate first wore Erdem when touring Canada back in 2011 – and the designer's gorgeously feminine styles have become a staple part of her wardrobe ever since.

Taken from his pre-fall collection, this particular dress cost £2,260 ($2,970) and boasted a highly complex piece of engineering, created using an array of angular seams, darts and inset pieces.

The gown was crafted from silk-gazar, a unique fabric which is made by weaving high-twist double yarns as one. Effectively a heavier silk with a satin finish that gives a dress form and fluidity, it is the same fabric that was used to make Kate's Sarah Burton for Alexander McQueen wedding gown.

Erdem has said this particular design collection of his was inspired by 1960s Japanese prints, a theme which can be seen throughout that entire line and most especially in the delectable pattern of Kate's dress – a vivid print known as "Ohana Tulip".

The gown also features a boat neckline – a favourite cut with Kate as it complements her slim collarbone – a V-neck back, and a gathered skirt with box pleats. Not all style commentators were taken with the unusual ruffled tier at the skirt's base, but others felt it added drama to the dress and worked well with Kate's statuesque height.

The Handbag and Shoes Kate picked out the black in the dress print by opting for her Anya Hindmarch "Maud" clutch purse in black satin. This £475 ($625) bag is a firm favourite that she has carried regularly since joining the Royal Family back in 2011. Handmade in one of the oldest purse frame workshops in England, the Maud was one of the first bags Hindmarch ever designed and has proved a popular choice for weddings and other formal occasions ever since. Made entirely from soft satin silk, the Maud can also be personalized with an embroidered monogram and embossed handwritten message for a truly special touch.

Kate also wore her £450 ($590) "Cosmic" suede 4.7-inch platform heels by Jimmy Choo – a style no longer available, but one that Kate has worn to many a red carpet event. The famous shoe designer does, however, still make a similar pair known as "Hope 100" with a slightly smaller 4-inch heel and more rounded toe for around £475 ($625).

The Jewellery For this formal occasion Kate was especially sparkling, starting with the stunning diamond bracelet commonly believed to be a gift from Prince Charles. The Duchess also debuted a vintage pair of earrings we'd not previously seen on her before. The sapphire and diamond drops originally belonged to the Queen Mother and are thought to have been passed on to Kate via the Queen – who inherited the entire jewellery collection following her mother's death in 2002.

Erdem Moralioglu The Duchess of Cambridge is an enormous fan of the award-winning Canadian fashion designer Erdem Moralioglu and has wowed in a number of his pieces in recent years. Having first sported the label, very deliberately, on the royal tour of Canada in 2011, Kate has seemed to delight in his pretty, patterned dresses and block colour coats ever since.

Erdem was born in Montreal, Canada, to a Turkish father and an English mother and grew up travelling between Canada and England. After working as an intern for British designer Vivienne Westwood, he moved to London in 2000 to study a Masters in Fashion at the Royal College of Art. He then worked in New York alongside Diane von Furstenberg, before returning to London to launch his own label in 2005, where he's remained ever since.

Well known for his experimental textiles and intricate craftsmanship as well as pretty, feminine, floral designs, Erdem has a coterie of high-profile clients alongside Kate, including Michelle Obama and Keira Knightley.

These days Erdem's influence filters down into the high street, where you will find a raft of Erdem-esque digitally-manipulated floral prints. He adores working with silk and lace to produce clothes steeped in echoes from the past, but which are crisply modern too – and very much the kind of clothes women want to wear.

Not interested in following trends as such, Erdem says he concentrates only on making women look and feel beautiful. "I never think about what's sexy," he told Australian *Vogue*. "I don't agonize over whether her bum will look big in something. I focus on the silhouettes and the proportions and hope that this takes care of everything."

ABOVE: A Royal legacy: Kate proudly wears the diamond and sapphire earrings passed down from the Queen Mother.

Look Fabulous in Big Florals

If the thought of wearing a trendy bold floral makes you want to wrap up in a big black coat, you are far from alone. Wearing a busy print like Kate's that's likely to draw attention can be intimidating – even for the most confident of women. The key thing to remember is that a floral print can be extremely flattering on all shapes – it's all about knowing how to make the trend work for you and sticking to a few basic rules.

Start simple
If you don't want to overpower with florals, stick to a dress or skirt with one large floral motif to begin with. This will give a neat nod to the modern trend without being too much.

Look out for secret panelling
Choose a dress or top with clever contouring that has all the print in the centre, with darker block panels on the outside. A trick favoured by many Hollywood stars on the red carpet, this optical illusion will slim you down in seconds.

Use it to hide flaws
Be clever with your pattern positioning and use florals to distract from any worrying areas. So, for example, if you feel top-heavy, keep the focus on the bottom half of your body by wearing the print there, and vice versa.

Go pale and interesting
For a softer finish, opt for a subtle floral print that isn't too graphic. Choose a colour that flatters your skin tone to keep the overall look more natural.

Work with your natural shape
If you've been graced with the gift of height, you can pull off larger prints, such as a floral maxidress or evening gown. But if you're on the petite side, full-length large prints can overwhelm your proportions. This doesn't mean forgoing bigger floral patterns completely, but sticking to a shorter above-the-knee skirt length will stop you looking swamped.

Indian Summer Style

The Dress Always a keen ambassador of international fashion on royal trips, the Duchess of Cambridge was quick to promote local designers throughout her tour of India in April 2016. For an engagement that included both a cricket match and tour of one of Mumbai's most deprived areas, Kate wore a delicately printed georgette dress by Indian designer Anita Dongre.

The vibrant "Gulrukh" dress – featuring coral, red and green Jaipur-inspired patterns – was straight off the catwalk, having been a key piece in the designer's Spring/Summer 2016 Love Notes collection at Lakmé Fashion Week in Mumbai – just one week before the royal tour.

Dongre, who started her label in 2009 and has eight clothing shops across India, told *The Telegraph* newspaper that Kate's stylist, Natasha Archer, had requested some clothes for the Duchess prior to the tour. However, Dongre had no idea beforehand whether her designs had made the cut. "It was a real surprise. I was at home when I saw the pictures and was so delighted," she says of seeing Kate in one of her pieces.

Perhaps even more surprising for Dongre was the fact that Kate's team had altered the original design from a full-length gown with a matching traditional shawl to a more Western look. "In India, a lot of woman would wear this with trousers and a stole," Dongre explained, "but Kate's stylist has taken the stole, converted part of it into a belt and then chopped it off so it can be worn as a dress." Thankfully, she was delighted with the adaption – "It looks easy, breezy and so contemporary and she looked beautiful," she told *The Telegraph*. Speaking for many people around the world, Dongre said of Kate, "I've always admired her sense of style. My clothes stand for a certain feminine elegance – I think she does the same."

In fact, in a savvy business move, Dongre quickly started offering Kate's customized version of the dress for around £175 ($230) – as well as still selling the original design. Of course, the by now famous "Kate effect" struck and Dongre's website was so inundated with orders from the UK and US it crashed.

Almost a year after wearing this dress, the Duchess went on to meet Anita Dongre in person at a reception dinner held at Buckingham Palace to mark the UK-India Year of Culture in February 2017. The designer tweeted about the event later that night, thrilled that Kate had chosen to wear a pair of her earrings to mark the occasion: "It was so lovely meeting The Duchess of Cambridge this evening. We chatted about our mutual love for Rajasthan and she chose to wear a pair of @anitadongrepinkcity earrings."

The Shoes To match the customized ethnic print dress, Kate chose a new pair of Monsoon "Fleur" wedges in taupe, costing £45 ($60). This was an apt choice as the UK high street store is known for its signature "Boho" look, created using beautiful fabrics, intricate prints and bold colours, with the inspiration and fabrics often sourced from eastern countries including India.

The Earrings To finish the look, Kate opted for more high-street-sourced accessories – this time a pair of filigree bead short drop earrings from Accessorize, costing just £8 ($10). The sister company to Monsoon, Accessorize is known for its delicate and often ethnic-inspired jewellery.

Superstylist: The Lowdown on Natasha Archer Although Kate continues to make all her own fashion choices, one member of staff who has become an invaluable style advisor in recent years is Natasha Archer. It is Natasha's job to call around the clothing labels Kate loves the most and obtain a suitable selection of garments for the Duchess to pick from before special events. Indeed, then aged just 29 years old, Natasha was dubbed "One of the most influential people in the fashion industry right now" by renowned style bible *Tatler* magazine in 2016.

The royal tour of India is a perfect example of Archer's industry and influence. For the Duchess of Cambridge to accompany Prince William to India and Bhutan, months of careful preparation went into ensuring every last detail of her travelling wardrobe was perfectly balanced. And while Kate was reportedly highly involved, planning a full royal tour is a huge task, which is where Archer comes into her own.

Known to friends and colleagues as "Tash", Archer began working at Kensington Palace as the Duchess's PA, but has added the role of stylist to her duties over the past few years, thanks to her great eye and similar sartorial sensibilities.

Archer's importance to Kate was first noted when she was snapped carrying a suitcase – believed to be full of outfit options – into the Lindo Wing of St Mary's Hospital immediately following Prince George's birth. In the years since, she has continued to receive credit for influencing Kate's fashion choices, supporting the Duchess as her style has evolved and become more daring and glamorous as she has grown in confidence.

Making Boho Chic Look Elegant

The trip to India gave Kate a perfect opportunity to embrace the boho look, a style that, in her own demure way, she obviously enjoys experimenting with from time to time. For the Duchess, boho usually means opting for floaty dresses, with vintage and ethnic-inspired accessories, and wearing her hair in natural, loose curls. Kate cleverly manages to evoke the essence of the look without descending into over-the-top "hippy" clichés – and so can you by following these tips …

Boho tends to work best as a summer look
Choose light clothing in natural fabrics such as cotton, linen, velvet, chiffon and silk for effortless flow.

Experiment with patterns
Ethnic-inspired patterns and soft floral prints work especially well with this look, as with Kate's Anita Dongre frock opposite.

Go for the maxi
Full-length, loose-fitting dresses set the tone perfectly – but team with a belt, as Kate does, to add some shape.

Dare to go bare
For shoes, leather and suede in natural shades such as beige, blush and tan are your best bet. To channel Kate's elegance, a pair of nude wedges or courts is ideal.

Dress for your body type
If you are curvier, look for items with more structure, as floaty layers can make you look bigger than you are. Similarly, if you are shorter, picking "midi" hemlines can prevent you looking lost in the clothing.

LOOK 47

Prints Charming

The Outfit In May 2016, the Duke and Duchess of Cambridge, along with Prince Harry, attended the launch of Heads Together – the royal trio's landmark campaign to end the stigma around mental health – at the Queen Elizabeth Olympic Park in London.

Proving herself the queen of smart-casual daywear, Kate looked elegant yet contemporary in this sleek printed skirt and top combination.

With Britain experiencing something of a heatwave during this particular week, Kate also managed to look chic while keeping cool in this winning "workwear" combination – which is no mean fashion feat.

The cream "Binky" blouse is by Goat – a brand that has become a firm daywear favourite with the Duchess over the years. The £290 ($380) garment is described by the company as: "A classic and beautifully crafted blouse that is a key building block of a capsule wardrobe". The understated yet pretty top has a round neck and full sleeves, which gather into cuffs with silk covered buttons.

The Duchess teamed the blouse with the Blue Geo Jacquard Midi Skirt by Banana Republic, marking the first time she had been spotted wearing the US retailer, which is owned by Gap. Sadly, by October of 2016 the brand announced it was closing its UK stores, although its clothes can still be bought online in the UK.

Priced £96 ($125), the cotton A-line skirt with a striking navy, black and cream geometric pattern hits mid-calf – a cut that chimes all the right fashion notes for Kate, with midi skirts very much in vogue for all of 2016.

The Shoes and Bag Kate carried her trusty £185 ($245) navy suede L.K. Bennett "Frome" clutch bag – a regular bag companion – and completed the look with her £425 ($560) navy suede Rupert Sanderson "Malory" pumps, which have a pointed toe and 4-inch heel and help add elegant length to the Duchess's shapely calves for this outfit.

The Jewellery To offset her elegant Cartier Ballon Bleu watch (see also page 168), Kate wore her much-loved sapphire and diamond oval drop "Diana" earrings. She was first spotted wearing these earrings when she and Prince William posed for an official portrait at Clarence House back in June 2011, just before their tour of North America. A gift from her husband, they were originally owned by the late Princess Diana as studs, which were then remodelled into drop earrings. They feature a single oval sapphire stone with a ring cluster of diamonds and dangle from a single diamond lever.

Getting Your Goat

Created by Jane Lewis in 2001, British clothing brand Goat specializes in luxury investment pieces and has quickly become known as a go-to brand for smart women's workwear. Starting as a cashmere company, Goat has since branched out to create a wide range of women's clothing.

Despite never once having staged a fashion show, over the last decade and a half Goat has quietly become an incredible success story. As well as the Duchess of Cambridge, the likes of Victoria Beckham, Kim Sears and Emilia Fox are all regular wearers of Goat's simple dresses, elegant blouses and smartly tailored jackets.

"I've tried very hard to be very discreet," Lewis told *The Telegraph* newspaper in a rare interview in 2016. "We don't show – we are not a bells and whistles company. It is much cooler and more chic to be under the radar. We have been dressing the great and good for a very long time."

As a designer, Lewis is entirely self-taught, having worked alongside designer Elspeth Gibson as an assistant for two years and learning on the job before deciding to branch out on her own. "I started Goat to address very real concerns, and provide those key basics which seem to be eternally elusive," she says. "The things we take for granted are the most difficult to find."

All of Goat's clothing is manufactured in Britain to the highest quality standards and so never creases, pulls or wears badly. Each garment is created as a timeless investment piece, rather than a trend-led item that will quickly date. "My motto is style over fashion, because style endures," Lewis told *The Telegraph*. "If you are a stylish person, you are likely to invest in pieces and wear them in your own way. I want to make future classics. Nothing would make me prouder than if someone digs out something of mine from their wardrobe that they bought four years ago and says 'I'm still wearing it!'"

Red and White Delight

The Dress When the Duchess stepped out in this eye-catching Alexander McQueen ensemble in September 2016 during her visit to Canada, its daring design features marked something of a shift from Kate's sometimes restrained royal tour style. But with her customary eye to diplomatic style signalling, the red and white colour palette of the ruffled £4,000 ($5,260) frock was a respectful nod to her host's national colours.

The custom-made dress by one of Kate's favourite British fashion houses featured red-embroidered eyelet detail, a tiered skirt with an unusual scalloped hem, a high collar, a white belt, and delicately painted buttons. Inspired by a dress from Sarah Burton's Resort 2017 collection for Alexander McQueen, Kate's bespoke version featured a more demure knee-length skirt – rather than the above-the-knee length of the original – and slimmer-fit sleeves with white cuffs rather than the more billowing, ruffled sleeves of Burton's catwalk version. However, Kate's design did showcase the key features – including the tiered skirt, pretty floral button detailing and a mandarin-style collar – in which Sarah Burton's whimsical theme for the collection can clearly be seen. It was a look the designer described as being inspired by: "the intricately beautiful floral patterns seen painted on gypsy caravans and canal barges in the British countryside." In picking this dress, Kate was not only returning to one of her most trusted designers, she was also going back to one of her favourite fabrics that we have seen her wear many times before – broderie anglaise. This pretty form of traditional embellishment embroidery incorporates fabric cutouts, eyelets and over-sewing and is often used to give clothes a traditional, romantic feel.

The Shoes and Bag Because the dress featured such a striking pattern, a safe bet would have been to go for neutral accessories to tone down the outfit. However, on this occasion an increasingly style-confident Kate shunned her favourite nude pumps and chose bold red shoes and a matching clutch that helped ensure the print really popped out. The £640 ($840) Miu Miu scarlet suede bag featured a bow detail and was described on fashion website Net-a-Porter as: "A ladylike style with a gilded silver chain." This was the first time Kate has been spotted with anything made by Miu Miu – the more youthful, hipper offshoot of Prada, named after Miuccia Prada's nickname. The matching crimson £165 ($215) "Pinpoint" heels from Russell and Bromley completed the striking rouge ensemble.

Looking Sensational in Scallops

The scallop edge, as seen on Kate's Alexander McQueen dress below, is named after the curved edge of a scallop's shell. The shape is essentially created by placing half-circle cutouts along any fabric edge, where they work to magically make a hemline look much less severe and add a dainty, demure touch to any outfit – as Kate demonstrated. Feminine and flirty, scalloped edges elevate wardrobe staples into something special. Better still, it doesn't matter what your body shape is, because scalloped edging is one of the most flattering trends around. Dressed up or dressed down, here are just a few ways to wear the trend with flair ...

On a skirt
Choose a skirt in a solid colour and a modern just-above-the-knee cut for a flirty, yet elegant feel.

On shorts or "skorts"
A wavy hemline in place of a straight one adds a whimsical feel to normally staid shorts.

On a dress
A rippling scalloped edge on a simple frock evokes thoughts of spring and breezy afternoons – without succumbing to overpowering flower power.

On a tunic top
The drapey fit of a tunic is flattering for all shapes, but choosing one with a scalloped hem and sleeve makes the overall look more sophisticated.

A suit
The subtleness of the scallop edge makes it a safe bet to wear to work, helping to soften a structured suit.

LOOK 49

Purple Reigns

The Dress For the final day of her royal visit to Germany in July 2017, Kate wore an outfit created for her by a very familiar name – Emilia Wickstead.

The New Zealand-born designer, whose modern take on traditional ladylike style has proved a hit with "in-the-know" socialites worldwide, has been behind many of the Duchess's formal looks for everything from garden parties at Buckingham Palace to royal tours and military engagements.

The lilac shade of this particular garment was a summery feminine spin on royal purple, in one of Kate's favourite silhouettes – the A-line dress. This time with long sleeves, a fitted top, nipped-in waist and flared skirt.

The outfit, which Kate wore to the Maritime Museum in Hamburg to celebrate the joint UK-Germany Year of Science, summed up the Duchess's entire wardrobe for this German tour – appropriate and elegant, while still flashing hints of the more fashion-forward flair edging its way into her look. Pale lilac isn't a shade Kate is often seen in – one notable exception being the stunning light purple Jenny Packham gown she wore to the 2011 BAFTAs – and many style experts consider it a tricky hue to pull off. But the shade of this dress was vibrant enough for the Duchess to avoid looking washed out, instead adding zing to her skin tone and offering a great contrast to her glossy dark locks.

The Shoes and Bag This classic dress was punctuated as ever with equally stylish accessories, but for once Kate chose not to match her shoe and bag colour, giving the overall look a more modern, edgier vibe. The russet snakeskin clutch by Anya Hindmarch nicely contrasts with her £500 ($660) Gianvito Rossi 105 suede heels in praline.

The Earrings The Duchess gave another outing to her £3,900 ($5,130) Kiki McDonough lavender amethyst pear and oval drop earrings, a gorgeous pair she debuted on her tour of India and Bhutan, earlier in 2016.

BELOW: Setting the tone: Kate and family coordinate perfectly in red and white for a trip to Warsaw, Poland.

Coordinating a Picture-Perfect Family

Kate's fashion credentials have been long established, but by the time of the German 2017 royal tour, it was clear that she had also mastered the art of seemingly effortless coordinated family dressing.

The Duke and Duchess of Cambridge, along with Prince George and Princess Charlotte, were spied in several colour-matched ensembles during their visit to Poland and Germany. In Warsaw, for example, the family was a symphony of red and white, Poland's national colours. The Duchess wore white Alexander McQueen, the Duke a navy suit, white shirt and red tie, Princess Charlotte a red-and-white smocked dress and red shoes, while Prince George sported a red-and-blue check shirt and navy shorts.

Then for the tour's last official engagement in Hamburg, the family toned perfectly in purple, mauve and pinks, with Kate's lilac Emilia Wickstead dress matching with Prince George, who sported a checked shirt in a similar tone. Princess Charlotte, meanwhile, was dressed in a pink summer dress with white socks and pink Mary Jane shoes. Even Prince William joined in with a plum-coloured tie. Wearing similar colour tones and clothing shapes in this way certainly makes the Royal Family look perfectly styled for all their official occasions and photos.

But how can us mere mortals match family members to create stylish photos without looking just a bit naff? These clever coordination tricks will have you dressing in perfect harmony …

Think tonal
What prevents the Cambridges' outfits from straying into the tacky side of the fashion spectrum is their use of tone. Picking colours from the same spectrum without being identical means the overall look ties together without being too "matchy-matchy". Try picking two main colours and then adding softer accent tones to complete your colour scheme.

Match intensity, not colour
Another foolproof way to coordinate outfits in a natural manner is to go for different colours, but at the same level of intensity. For example, all primary colours or all pastels.

Lay your clothes out beforehand
Seeing them all next to each other will give you a good idea of how the pieces will look as an ensemble – so you can easily see which items work and which ones don't.

Location, location, location
When taking a special set of family photos, it's important to consider your surroundings. Are you going to be on the beach, where there are plenty of neutral tones? Or under a tree surrounded by bright foliage? The key is to then select a colour palette for your outfits that will complement the setting rather than try to compete with it.

Pick timeless outfits
If all else fails, stay simple and classic. Styles come and go, but photos last forever, so avoid anything that is too "of the moment".

Poppies to Remember

The Dress On August 30, 2017, just five days before the official announcement from Kensington Palace that she was expecting her third child, the Duchess of Cambridge was pictured arriving at the White Garden at Kensington Palace with the Princes William and Harry. They were there to pay tribute to Princess Diana on the eve of the 10th anniversary of her tragic death, at a newly planted garden created in her memory.

The pretty garden featured flowers and foliage inspired by memories of the Princess's life, image and style, and was filled with white roses, narcissi and forget-me-nots.

To mark the occasion, Kate wore an outfit that paid perfect tribute to the woman she sadly never had the honour of meeting. With its high neck and pussy bow, Kate's teal floral dress was poignantly evocative of some of the outfits Diana wore during the early 1980s. The Prada dress was also decorated in red poppies, a plant long associated with remembrance and consolation. In Greek mythology, the God of Death Thanatos is sometimes depicted wearing a crown of poppies and, of course, nowadays the flower is most noted for its role in Remembrance Day, to commemorate soldiers who have died in war. The £1,420 ($1870) dress was made from lightweight silk-crepe and featured a full skirt, shirred waistline, long sleeves and a self-tie neck bow.

The Shoes and Earrings Kate paired the Prada dress with her trusty £195 ($255) L.K. Bennett "Fern" heels in "trench" colour – the classic nude court shoes she so often favours, as they go with everything and never compete with the main outfit. She also chose to wear her Monica Vinader "Siren Wire Green" £135 ($175) earrings, which picked out the green of her silk frock perfectly.

The Umbrella On this rather damp day, Kate chose to carry a Brigg umbrella – a practical accessory made by British heritage brand Swaine Adeney Brigg. The company is famous for its high-quality products and has been supplying the upper echelons of British society, including royalty and prime ministers, with fine umbrellas and leather goods since 1750. According to the boast on Brigg's own website: "Today, we are still crafting reputedly the best umbrellas in the world in our workrooms in England!" The Duchess selected the smaller, ladies' design with a maple wood handle, brown canopy and gold-plated collar, retailing at around £325 ($425).

Saying it with Flowers

The thoughtful Prada floral tribute of remembrance to Princess Diana on the previous page was not the first time the Duchess of Cambridge had used the language of flowers to convey important messages. This long tradition dates back to the Victorian age when each flower was said to have a special meaning. If there's any doubt that Kate's floral signalling is deliberate, consider that her wedding day bouquet was designed by Shane Connolly – a British master florist who wrote a book entitled *Discovering the Meaning of Flowers*. On that auspicious occasion, Kate's carefully thought-out all-white bridal bunch contained the following floral missives:

Lily of the valley: According to the language of flowers, this delicate bloom represents trustworthiness – a good characteristic for any husband or wife to have. It's also strongly associated with the return of happiness.

Ivy: An appropriate choice as it stands for fidelity, friendship, and affection.

Sweet William: This flower represents gallantry, but was also chosen, of course, as a nod to Kate's husband-to-be, who shares the same name.

Hyacinth: These delicately scented blooms symbolize the constancy of love.

Myrtle: This flower's special meaning is as an emblem of true love and every royal bride since Queen Victoria has carried a sprig of myrtle in her wedding bouquet. Interestingly, this myrtle is traditionally picked from a very special place – Queen Victoria's own 170-year-old garden at Osborne House on the Isle of Wight, from a tree the monarch herself planted in 1845!

Following the wedding, in another nod to history, the Duchess of Cambridge sent her bouquet back to Westminster Abbey to rest on the Grave of the Unknown Warrior. This particular tradition was started by the late Queen Mother in memory of her brother Fergus who died in the First World War.

Mum's the Word

With the eyes of the world upon you, it's never easy to keep a new pregnancy under wraps until you are ready to announce it – especially if you are suffering from the severe form of morning sickness known as hyperemesis gravidarum that has plagued Kate for each of her three pregnancies. But third time around Kate was a seasoned professional at staying chic while deftly drawing the eyes of the world's press away from her burgeoning bump. Indeed, plenty of the tricks she employed are easy to follow, should you ever want to avoid awkward questions or simply minimize your own bump.

In the weeks leading up to her baby announcement, Kate avoided figure-fitting clothing, opting instead for more structured coat dresses and ruffle waist details. For example, while on royal tour of Poland and Germany, she concealed changes in her frame by opting for peplum skirts and dresses and studiously hid her waist under blazers.

But it wasn't all distracting dresses – for a day's rowing, Kate made the clever pick of a loose Breton-style striped top – which didn't nip in at the waist – over a pair of stretchy jeans.

For eveningwear, Kate chose outfits that drew attention toward her neckline – and therefore away from her waist – such as the V-neck ivory cocktail dress by designer Gosia Baczyńska she wore in Poland. Not only was the low neck eye-catching, Kate teamed it with a chunky pearl necklace that was sure to be everyone's focus.

A little later in July 2017, while she attended a series of Passchendaele commemorations in Belgium with Prince William, Kate kept any signs of her changing figure hidden beneath a variety of clever coat dresses.

Finally, at the end of August, with the announcement just days away, she understood that the large pussy-bow detail at the neck of her green floral Prada dress (page 191) was a good way to draw the eye well above belly height.

Sadly, after the pregnancy was announced on September 4, Kate's extreme morning sickness meant many of her upcoming engagements had to be cancelled – leaving her fashion fans to wait a little longer than usual for her next style statement.

OPPOSITE ABOVE: Hidden meanings: Kate's pretty white wedding bouquet drew on the traditional romantic symbolism of certain flowers.

OPPOSITE BELOW: The art of distraction: The deep V of Kate's Gosia Baczyńska dress and bold pearl necklace meant nobody noticed her tiny pregnancy bump in Poland, July 2017.

RIGHT: Hanging loose: This relaxed Breton top, worn during a boat ride in Heidelberg, Germany, July 2017, helped hide Kate's third pregnancy before it was officially announced.

Kate's Style Directory

Want to know where Kate buys her jeans or where to find her go-to shops and labels for formal and casual wear? Our handy and extensive directory lists the key stores and where to locate them.

As with the 50 classic looks on the previous pages, one of the attributes that propels Kate from simply stylish into style icon territory is her ability to put together a complete outfit. Not only does she choose beautiful dresses, elegant coats and chic separates, but she also pays careful attention to every last detail and knows how to pick the perfect accessory. Whether it is choosing the ideal Kiki McDonough topaz earrings to finish off a look, the note-perfect L.K. Bennett clutch bag or some on-theme R. Soles cowboy boots, Kate has the eye of a professional stylist and here we list her beloved accessories brands as well as her all-time high-street favourites such as Reiss, Whistles and Zara, plus a few of her lesser-known haunts, including Episode at House of Fraser and Russell & Bromley.

The list, of course, wouldn't be Kate's unless it included her designer labels of choice, such as Alexander McQueen, Alice Temperley, Emilia Wickstead and Issa. And for those finishing touches, we detail where to get your hands on items from her make-up brands to her perfume of choice.

Accessories

Aquatalia by Marvin K
UK
Russell & Bromley
24–25 New Bond Street
London W1S 2PS
08450 342259
www.russellandbromley.co.uk

USA
Neiman Marcus
Maple & Paulding Avenue
White Plains
New York NY 10601
914-428-2000
www.neimanmarcus.com

Saks Fifth Avenue
611 5th Avenue
New York NY 10022
877-551-7257
www.saksfifthavenue.com

Australia
Diana's of Noosa
Bay Village
26 Hastings Street
Noosa Heads QL 4567
07-5447-5991
www.dianasofnoosa.com.au

Raymond Poulton Shoes
Shop 110, Rundle Mall
Myer Centre
Adelaide SA 5000
08-8410-6998
www.raymondpoulton.com.au

Stuart Weitzman for Hermanns
Shop G061
Chadstone Shopping Centre
1341 Dandenong Road
Chadstone VIC 3148
03-9522-9736
www.hermanns.com.au/
Hermanns.asp

Stuart Weitzman for Hermanns
175 Collins Street
Melbourne VIC 3000
03-9522-9709
www.hermanns.com.au/
Hermanns.asp

Stuart Weitzman for Hermanns
Shop 3020 Westfield Sydney
188 Pitt Street
Sydney NSW 2000
02-8424-2737
www.hermanns.com.au/
Hermanns.asp

Canada
Available at many independent
retailers throughout the country,
including the following:

Brown's Shoes
3035 Boul. Carrefour Laval
Laval, QC H7T 1C7
450-681-4924
www.brownsshoes.com

Brown's Shoes
1 Promenade Circle
Thornhill ON L4J 4P8
905-764-1444
www.brownsshoes.com

Brown's Shoes
300 Borough Drive
Scarborough ON M1P 4P5
416-290-5158
www.brownsshoes.com

Davids
Markio Designs Inc.
1200 Bay Street
Toronto ON M5R 2A5
416-929-9629
www.davidsfootwear.com

Holt Renfrew
2452 Laurier Boulevard
Quebec City QC G1V 2L1
418-656-6783
www.holtrenfrew.com

Holt Renfrew
737 Dunsmuir Street
Vancouver BC V7Y 1E4
604-681-3121
www.holtrenfrew.com

Jean-Paul Fortin
2050 De Celles
Quebec G2C 1X8
418-845-5369
www.jeanpaulfortin.com

Ogilvy
1307 Sainte-Catherine Street W.
Montreal QC H3G 1P7
514-842-7711
www.ogilvycanada.com

Le Chameau
UK
Bestboots Ltd
Coates Farm
Nettleton
Wiltshire SN14 7NS
01249 783530
www.bestboots.co.uk

Cedarstone Limited
Callimore Farm
Droitwich
Worcestershire WR9 0NS
01299 851767
www.le-chameau-clothing.co.uk

John Norris of Penrith
21 Victoria Road
Penrith
Cumbria CA11 8HP
01768 864211
www.johnnorris.co.uk

Out of the City Ltd
Ordnance Road
Buckshaw Village
Chorley
Lancashire PR7 7EL
0845 862 4624
www.outofthecity.co.uk

Philip Morris & Son
21 Widemarsh Street
Hereford HR4 9EE
01432 377089
www.philipmorrisdirect.co.uk

Jimmy Choo
UK
32 Sloane Street
London SW1X 9NR
020 7823 1051
www.jimmychoo.com

27 New Bond Street
London W1S 2RH
020 7493 5858
www.jimmychoo.com

USA
240 North Rodeo Drive
Beverly Hills
Los Angeles CA 90210
310-860-9045
www.jimmychoo.com

Bloomingdale's
845 Market Street
San Francisco CA 94103
415-856-5431
www.jimmychoo.com

716 Madison Avenue
New York NY 10065
212-759-7078
www.jimmychoo.com

Australia
Chadstone Shopping Centre
1341 Dandenong Road
Chadstone VIC 3148
61-0-39038-10-84
www.jimmychoo.com

MLC Centre
41 Castlereagh Street
Sydney NSW 2000
61-2-8666-06-06
www.jimmychoo.com

Westfield Bondi Junction
500 Oxford Street
Bondi Junction NSW 2022
61-2-9078-86-68
www.jimmychoo.com

Jane Corbett
UK
Roxtons
10/11 Bridge Street
Hungerford
Berkshire RG17 0EH
07557 868260
www.janecorbett.co.uk
(Studio visits by appointment only)

Episode
UK
House of Fraser
318 Oxford Street
London W1C 1HF
0845 602 1073
www.houseoffraser.co.uk

Salvatore Ferragamo
UK
24 Old Bond Street
London W1S 4AL
020 7629 5007
www.ferragamo.com

207 Sloane Street
London SW1X 9QX
020 7838 7730
www.ferragamo.com

Westfield
London W12 7SL
020 8743 0212
www.ferragamo.com

Harrods
87–135 Brompton Road
London SW1X 0NA
020 7730 1234
www.ferragamo.com

Mitsukoshi
14–20 Lower Regent Street
London SW1Y 4PH
020 7839 6714
www.ferragamo.com

Selfridges
400 Oxford Street
London W1A 1AB
020 7318 2326
www.ferragamo.com

USA
655 5th Ave
New York NY 10022
212-759-3822
www.ferragamo.com

45 North Michigan Avenue
Chicago IL 60611
312-397-0464
www.ferragamo.com

8500 Beverly Boulevard No. 770
Los Angeles CA 90048
310-652-0279
www.ferragamo.com

100 Huntington Avenue
Boston MA 02116
617-859-4924
www.ferragamo.com

Australia
David Jones
100 Rundle Mall
Adelaide SA 5000
61-8-8305-3269
www.ferragamo.com

45 Collins Street
Melbourne VIC 3000
61-3-9654-5066
www.ferragamo.com

45 Castlereagh Street
Sydney NSW 2000
61-2-9221-3036
www.ferragamo.com

Sylvia Fletcher for James Lock
UK
Lock & Co. Hatters
6 St James's Street
London SW1A 1EF
020 7930 8874
www.lockhatters.co.uk

French Sole Ltd
UK
26 Brook Street
London W1K 5DQ
020 7493 2678
www.frenchsole.com

6 Ellis Street
London SW1X 9AL
020 7730 3771
www.frenchsole.com

323 King's Road
London SW3 5EP
020 7351 1634
www.frenchsole.com

61 Marylebone Lane
London W1U 2PA
020 7486 0021
www.frenchsole.com

Givenchy Sunglasses
UK
Dover Street Market
17–18 Dover Street
London W1S 4LT
020 7518 0680
www.givenchy.com

Harrods
87–135 Brompton Road
London SW1X 7XL
020 7730 1234
www.givenchy.com

Harvey Nichols
109–125 Knightsbridge
London SW1X 7RJ
020 7235 5000
www.givenchy.com

USA
Barneys New York
660 Madison Avenue
New York NY 10021
212-826-8900
www.givenchy.com

Bergdorf Goodman
754 5th Avenue
New York NY 10019
212-753-7300
www.givenchy.com

Jeffrey
449 West 14th Street
New York NY 10014
212-206-1272
www.givenchy.com

Canada
Holt Renfrew
50 Bloor Street
Toronto M4W 1A1
416-922-2333
www.givenchy.com

La Maison Simon
977 Sainte-Catherine Ouest
Montreal QC H3B 4W3
514-282-1840
www.givenchy.com

SSense
9600 Meilleur
Montreal QC H2N 2ES
514-384-1906
www.givenchy.com

Anya Hindmarch
UK
15–17 Pont Street
London SW1X 9EH
020 7838 9177
www.anyahindmarch.com

63 Ledbury Road
London W11 2AJ
020 7792 4427
www.anyahindmarch.com

118 New Bond Street
London W1S 1EW
020 7493 1628
www.anyahindmarch.com

157–158 Sloane Street
London SW1X 9AB
020 7730 0961
www.anyahindmarch.com

USA
29 East 60th Street
New York NY 10022
212-750-3974
www.anyahindmarch.com

118 South Robertson Boulevard
Los Angeles CA 90048
310-271-9707
www.anyahindmarch.com

Jaeger
UK
200–206 Regent Street
London W1R 6BN
020 7979 1100
www.jaeger.co.uk

102 George Street
Edinburgh EH2 3DF
0131 225 8811
www.jaeger.co.uk

20 Milsom Street
Bath
Avon BA1 1DE
01225 466415
www.jaeger.co.uk

Kiki McDonough
UK
12 Symons Street
London SW3 2TJ
020 7730 3323
www.kiki.co.uk

Also available through Astley
Clarke: www.astleyclarke.com

L.K. Bennett
UK
164–166 King's Road
London SW3 4UR
020 7351 9659
www.lkbennett.com

94 Marylebone High Street
London W1U 4RY
020 7224 0319
www.lkbennett.com

45–45a George Street
Edinburgh EH2 2HT
0131 226 3370
www.lkbennett.com

Victoria Square
Belfast BT1 4QG
02890 238 292
www.lkbennett.com

St Davids Two
Tregegar Street
Cardiff CF10 2FB
029 2034 1143
www.lkbennett.com

USA
Bloomingdale's
59th Street & Lexington Avenue
New York NY 10022
212-705-2000
www.lkbennett.com

900 North Michigan Avenue
Chicago IL 60611
312-374-0958

8100 Tysons Corner Center
McLean VA 22102
703-556-4600

Houston Galleria
5085 Westheimer Road
Houston TX 77056
713-961-0009
www.lkbennett.com

Miu Miu
UK
185 Sloane Street
London SW1X 9QP
020 7235 6965
www.miumiu.com

House of Fraser
21–45 Buchanan Street
Glasgow G1 3HL

USA
1000 Third Avenue
New York, NY 10022
212-705-2824

Pied à Terre
UK
House of Fraser
318 Oxford Street
London W1C 1HF
0845 602 1073
www.houseoffraser.co.uk

Prada
UK
16–18 Old Bond Street
London W1S 4PS
020 7647 5000
www.prada.com

House of Fraser
11–45 Buchanan Street
Glasgow G1 3HL
0844 800 3728
www.prada.com

Selfridges & Co.
1 Exchange Square
Manchester M31BD
0161 838 0710
www.prada.com

USA
312 South Galena Street
Aspen CO 81611
970-925-7001
www.prada.com

8500 Beverly Boulevard
Space 739
Beverly Hills CA 90048
310-228-1400
www.prada.com

3200 Las Vegas Boulevard South
Las Vegas NV 89109
702-699-7106
www.prada.com

Australia
David Jones
86–108 Castlereagh Street
Sydney NSW 2000
61-2-9266-5249
www.prada.com

Shop 1, The Moroccan
11 Elkhorn Avenue
Surfers Paradise QLD 4217
61-7-5539-8858
www.prada.com

75–77 Collins Street
Melbourne VIC 3000
61-03-96630978
www.prada.com

Canada
Holt Renfrew
510 8th Avenue SW
Calgary AB T2P 4HG
1-403-269-7341
www.prada.com

Holt Renfrew
737 Dunsmuir Street
Vancouver V7Y E4
1-604-681-3121
www.prada.com

Gianvito Rossi
UK
Harrods
87-135 Brompton Road
Knightsbridge
London SW1X 7XL
+44 (0)20 7730 1234
www.net-a-porter.com

USA
Barneys New York
660 Madison Avenue
New York NY
212-826-8900

R. Soles
UK
109A King's Road
London SW3 4PA
020 7351 5520
www.rsoles.com

Rupert Sanderson
UK
19 Bruton Place
London W1J 6LZ
020 7491 2260
www.rupertsanderson.com

2a Hans Road
London SW3 1RX
020 7584 9249
www.rupertsanderson.com

Emmy Scarterfield
UK
Emmy Shoes
65 Cross Street
London N1 2BB
020 7704 0012
www.emmyshoes.co.uk

Smithbilt Hats (Stetsons)
Canada
1103 12th Street Southeast
Calgary AB T2G 3H7
403-244-9131
www.smithbilthats.com

Jane Taylor Millinery
UK
3 Filmer Mews
75 Filmer Road
London SW6 7JF
020 8393 2333
www.janetaylormillinery.com

Stuart Weitzman
Canada
3035 Boulevard le Carrefour
Laval QC H7T 1C8
450-973-1468
http://uk.stuartweitzman.com

Chinook Center
6455 Macleod Trail SW
Calgary AB T2H 0K9
403-265-0551
http://uk.stuartweitzman.com

2305 Rockland
Mont-Royal QC H3P 3E9
514-735-6344
http://uk.stuartweitzman.com

Wilbur & Gussie
UK
Fenwick
63 New Bond Street
London W1S 1RJ
020 7629 9161
www.wilburandgussie.com

Liberty
Regent Street
London W1B 5AH
020 7734 1234
www.wilburandgussie.com

Ireland
Harvey Nichols Dublin
Dundrum Town Centre
Dublin 16
+353 (0) 1291 0488
www.wilburandgussie.com

USA
Gywnn's of Mount Pleasant
916 Houston Northcutt Blvd
Mt. Pleasant SC 29464
843-884-9518
www.wilburandgussie.com

Mildred Hoit
265 Sunrise Avenue
Palm Beach FL 334 80
561-833-6010
www.wilburandgussie.com

Vivi Shoes
503 West Lancaster Avenue
Wayne PA 19087
610-688-6732
www.wilburandgussie.com

High Street & Designer

Alexander McQueen
UK
4–5 Old Bond Street
London W1S 4PD
020 7355 0088
www.alexandermcqueen.com
USA
417 West 14th Street
New York NY 10014
212-645-1797
www.alexandermcqueen.com
8379 Melrose Ave
Los Angeles CA 90069
323-782-4983
www.alexandermcqueen.com

Bal Harbour
9700 Collins Avenue
Miami FLA 33154
305-866-2839
www.alexandermcqueen.com

Amanda Wakeley
UK
175–177 Fulham Road
London SW3 6JW
020 7352 7143
www.amandawakeley.com

Harvey Nichols
109–125 Knightsbridge
London SW1X 7RJ
020 7235 5000
www.amandawakeley.com

Harvey Nichols
107–111 Briggate Street
Leeds LS1 6AZ
0113 245 8119
www.amandawakeley.com

Harvey Nichols
30–34 St Andrews Square
Edinburgh EH2 3AD
0131 524 8388
www.amandawakeley.com

Harvey Nichols
21 New Cathedral Street
Manchester M3 1RE
0161 828 8864
www.amandawakeley.com

Anita Dongre
India
Everest Classic, Linking Rd, Khar
(West), Mumbai 400052 India
Tel No: +91 7045669647
www.anitadongre.com
Worldwide shipping
+91 9223355122

Banana Republic
UK
224 Regent Street
London W1B 3BR
020 7758 3550
www.bananarepublic.co.uk

23 King's Road
Duke of York Square
London SW3 4LY
020 7730 4704
www.bananarepublic.co.uk

24–26 Union Street
Bath BA1 1RS
01225 429559
www.bananarepublic.co.uk

The Trafford Centre
Manchester M17 8BN
0161 748 4613
www.bananarepublic.co.uk

USA
552 Broadway
New York NY 10012
212-334-2109
http://bananarepublic.gap.com

Beulah London
UK
14 Grosvenor Crescent
London SW1X 7EE
020 7235 3818
www.beulahlondon.com

Harvey Nichols
109–125 Knightsbridge
London SW1X 7RJ
020 7235 5000
www.beulahlondon.com

Kim Vine
84 The High Street
Marlborough
Wiltshire SN8 1HF
01672 519937
www.beulahlondon.com

USA
No stockists but will ship abroad.

Christopher Kane
UK
Browns
6c Sloane Street
London SW1X 9LE
020 7514 0040
www.brownsfashion.com

Question Air
129 Church Road
London SW13 9HR
020 8741 0816
www.question-air.com

USA
Barneys
3325 Las Vegas Boulevard South
Las Vegas NV 89109
702-629-4200
www.barneys.com

Emilia Wickstead
UK
28 Cadogan Place
London SW1X 9RX
020 7235 1104
www.emiliawickstead.com

Erdem
U.K. and Ireland
Selfridges
400 Oxford Street
London W1A 1AB
020 7318 2326
www.erdem.co.uk

Thomas Brown
88–95 Grafton Street
Dublin 2
+353 (0) 1605 6666
www.erdem.co.uk

USA
Barney's New York
9570 Wilshire Blvd.
Beverly Hills CA 90212
310-276-4400
www.erdem.co.uk

Saks Fifth Avenue
384 Post Street
San Francisco CA 94108
415-086-4300
www.erdem.co.uk

Canada
Holt Renfrew
1300 Rue Sherbrooke Ouest
Montreal QC H3G 1H9
514-842-5111
www.erdem.co.uk

50 Bloor Street W
Toronto ON M4W 3L8
416-922-2333
www.erdem.co.uk

Goat Fashion
UK
4 Conduit Street
London W1
020 7493 9323
www.goatfashion.com

Goldsign
UK
Selfridges
400 Oxford Street
London W1A 1AB
020 7318 2326
http://www.gold-sign-jeans.com

Hobbs
UK
37 Brompton Road
London SW3 1DE
020 7225 2137
www.hobbs.co.uk

115 High Street
Oxford OX1 4BX
01865 249 437
www.hobbs.co.uk
37 George Street
Richmond
London TW9 1HY
020 8948 6720
www.hobbs.co.uk

Hudson
UK
Mee
9a Bartlett Street
Bath BA1 2QZ
01225 442250
www.hudsonjeans.com
Mottoo
12 Duke Street
Brighton BN1 1AH
01273 326 633
www.hudsonjeans.com

Trilogy
63 Weymouth Street
London W1G 8NU
020 7486 8085
www.hudsonjeans.com

Australia
Mrs Watson
155 Sailors Bay Road
Northbridge NSW 2063
612-9958-1516
www.hudsonjeans.com

Momento
4 Manuka Circle
Manuka
Canberra ACT 2603
612-6295-1146
www.hudsonjeans.com

Page One
273 George Street
Sydney City NSW 2000
612-9252-6895
www.hudsonjeans.com

Issa
UK
12 Lots Road
London SW10 OQD
020 7352 4241
www.issalondon.com

89 Eastbourne Mews
London W2 6LQ
020 7262 3124
www.issalondon.com
Harrods
87–135 Brompton Road
London SW1X 7XL
020 7730 1234
www.issalondon.com

USA
Net-A-Porter
www.net-a-porter.com

J Brand
UK
House of Fraser,
Stores throughout the UK,
including:
318 Oxford Street
London W1C 1HF
0845 602 1073
www.houseoffraser.co.uk

USA
Suite 1D
811 Traction Ave
Los Angeles CA 90013
213-620-9797
www.jbrandjeans.com

40 Grants Ave
San Francisco CA 94108
415-982-5726
www.jbrandjeans.com

Australia
Debs
24 Ocean Beach Road
Sorrento VIC 3943
03-5984-1617
www.jbrandjeans.com

Mazal
Shop 2002
Westfield Sydney City
Sydney NSW 2022
61-404-875-111
www.jbrandjeans.com

Canada
Aritzia
701 West George Street
Vancouver BC V7Y 1AL
604-681-9301
www.jbrandjeans.com

Jenny Packham
UK
3a Carlos Place (ready-to-wear)
London W1K 3AN
020 7493 6295
www.jennypackham.com

75 Elizabeth Street (bridal, by
appointment only)
London SW1W 9PJ
020 7730 2264
www.jennypackham.com

34 Elizabeth Street (accessories)
London SW1W 9NZ
020 7730 4883
www.jennypackham.com

USA
Gabriella New York
400 W 14th Street
New York NY 10014
212-206-1915
www.jennypackham.com

Katherine Hooker
UK
19 Ashburnham Road
London SW10 0PG
020 7352 5091
www.katherinehooker.com

Libélula
UK
Austique
330 King's Road
London SW3 5UR
020 7376 3663
www.libelula-studio.com

Austique
40 New Cavendish Street
London W1G 8UD
020 7487 3468
www.libelula-studio.com

Katherine Bird
20 Battersea Rise
London SW11 1EE
020 7228 2235
www.libelula-studio.com

Katie and Jo
253 New King's Road
London SW6 4RB
020 7736 5304
www.libelula-studio.com

L.K. Bennett
(see Accessories, page 165)

M by Missoni
UK
Harrods
87–135 Brompton Road
London SW1X 7XL
020 7730 1234
www.m-missoni.com

Harvey Nichols
109–125 Knightsbridge
London SW1X 7RJ
020 7235 5000
www.m-missoni.com

USA
Neiman Marcus
737 North Michigan Avenue
Chicago IL 60611
1-31-2642 5900
www.m-missoni.com

Saks Fifth Avenue
9634 Wilshire Boulevard
Beverly Hills CA 90212
1-310-275-4211
www.m-missoni.com

Australia
Cyberia
579 Chapel Street
South Yarra
Melbourne VIC 41059
61-3-9824-1339
www.m-missoni.com

Spence & Lyda
Surry Hills
Sydney NSW 2010
61-2-921-26747
www.m-missoni.com

Canada
Holt Renfrew
25 The West Mallon
Toronto M9C 1B8
416-621-9900
www.m-missoni.com

Matthew Williamson
UK
28 Bruton Street
London W1J 6QH
020 7629 6200
www.matthewwilliamson.com

USA
415 West 14th Street
New York NY 10014
212-255-9881
www.matthewwilliamson.com

Mulberry
UK
26 Multrees Walk
Edinburgh EH1 3DQ
0131 557 5439
www.mulberry.com

House of Fraser
32–48 Promenade
Cheltenham GL50 1HP
0844 800 3715
www.mulberry.com

USA
Tysons Galleria
2001 International Drive
Mclean VA 22102
888-685-6856
www.mulberry.com

166 Grant Avenue
San Francisco CA 94108
888-685-6856
www.mulberry.com

Australia
Westfield Shopping Centre
188 Pitt Street
Sydney NSW 2000
61-28246-9160
www.mulberry.com

Penelope Chilvers
UK
The Cross
141 Portland Road
London W11 4LR
020 7727 6760
www.penelopechilvers.com

Lynx
20 West Park
Harrogate
North Yorkshire HG1 1BJ
01423 523845
www.penelopechilvers.com

USA
Erica Wilson
25–27 Main Street
Nantucket MA 02554
508-228-988
www.penelopechilvers.com

The Gallerie
520 E Durant Ave 102
Aspen CO 81611
970-544-4893
www.penelopechilvers.com

Project D
UK
Austique Chelsea
330 King's Road
London SW3 5UR
020 7376 4555
www.projectdlondon.com

Matches
13 Hill Street
Richmond
London TW9 1SX
0845 602 5612
www.projectdlondon.com

Square
15 Old Bond Street
Bath BA1 1BP
01225 464 997
www.projectdlondon.com

Australia
David Jones
86–108 Castlereagh Street
Sydney NSW 2000
02-9266-5544
www.davidjones.com.au

Emilio Pucci
UK
170 Sloane Street
London SW1X 9QG
020 7201 8171
http://home.emiliopucci.com

Harrods
87–135 Brompton Road
London SW1X 0NA
020 7730 1234
http://home.emiliopucci.com

Selfridges
400 Oxford Street
London W1A 1AB
020 7318 3369
http://home.emiliopucci.com

USA
Crystals at City Centre
3720 Las Vegas Boulevard South
Las Vegas NV 89158
702-262-9671
http://home.emiliopucci.com

Saks Fifth Avenue
611 5th Avenue
New York NY 10022
212-753-4000
http://home.emiliopucci.com

Ralph Lauren
UK
1 New Bond Street
London W1S 3RL
020 7535 4600
www.ralphlauren.co.uk

105–109 Fulham Road
London SW3 6RL
020 7590 7990
www.ralphlauren.co.uk

233–235 Westbourne Grove
London W11 2SE
020 7313 7590
www.ralphlauren.co.uk

USA
109 Prince Street
New York NY 10012
212-625-1660
www.ralphlauren.com

2040 Fillmore Street
San Francisco CA 94115
415-440-6536
www.ralphlauren.com

Australia
David Jones
80–108 Castlereagh Street
Sydney NSW 2000
01-02-9266-5581
www.ralphlauren.com

Reiss
UK
26 Trinity Street
Cambridge CB2 1TB
01223 308 733
www.reiss.com
114 King's Road
London SW3 4TX
020 7589 0439
www.reiss.com

10 Hampstead High Street
London NW3 1PX
020 7435 1542
www.reiss.com

USA
900 North Michigan Avenue
Chicago IL 60611
312-440-4460
www.reiss.com

Beverly Center
Bloomingdale's
8500 Beverly Boulevard
Los Angeles CA 90048
310-360-2700
www.reiss.com

309–313 Bleecker Street
New York NY 10014
212-488-2411
www.reiss.com

Roksanda Ilincic
UK
Browns
23–27 South Moulton Street
London W1K 5RD
020 7514 0016
www.roksandailincic.com

Flannels
Crown Square
Spinningfields
Manchester M3 3FL
0161 832 5536
www.roksandailincic.com

68–78 Vicar Lane
Leeds LS1 7JH
0113 234 9977
www.roksandailincic.com

USA
Elizabeth Charles
2056 Fillmore Street
San Francisco CA 94115
415-440-2100
www.roksandailincic.com

Kirna Zabete
96 Greene Street
New York NY 10012
212-941-9656
www.roksandailincic.com

Opening Ceremony
451 North La Cienega Boulevard
Los Angeles CA 90048
310-652-1120
www.roksandailincic.com
Australia
Cactus Jam
729 Glenferrie Road
Hawthorn VIC 3122
61-03-9819-0348
www.roksandailincic.com

Canada
Milli
310 Main Street West
Hamilton ON L8P 1J8
1-888-527-1531
www.roksandailincic.com

The Room – Hudson Bay
176 Yonge Street
Toronto ON M5C 2L7
1-416-861-9111
www.roksandailincic.com

Smythe
UK
Square One
43 St Johns Wood
London NW8 7NJ
020 7586 8658
www.smythelesvestes.com

Trilogy
33 Duke of York Square
London SW3 4LY
020 7730 6515
www.smythelesvestes.com

Rocca Boutique
32 Montpellier Parade
Harrogate
North Yorkshire HG1 2TG
01423 564146
www.smythelesvestes.com

USA
Ooh La Shoppe
25 The Plaza
Locust Valley
New York NY 11560
516-801-2700
www.smythelesvestes.com

Ron Herman
325 North Beverly Drive
Beverly Hills CA 90210
310-550-0910
www.smythelesvestes.com

Saks Fifth Avenue
9600 Wilshire Boulevard
Beverly Hills CA 90212
310-275-4211
www.smythelesvestes.com

Canada
Coup Boutique
10137 104 Street Northwest
Edmonton AB T5J 0Z9
1-780-756-3032
www.smythelesvestes.com
Holt Renfrew
240 Sparks Street
Ottawa ON K1P 6C9
1-613-238-2200
www.smythelesvestes.com

Ssense
90 Rue Saint Paul Ouest
Montreal QC H2Y 3S5
1-514-289-1906
www.smythelesvestes.com

Stella McCartney
UK
30 Bruton Street
London W1J 6QR
020 7518 3100
www.stellamccartney.com

91–95 Fulham Road
London SW3 6RH
020 7589 0092
www.stellamccartney.com

Selfridges
400 Oxford Street
London W1A 1AB
020 7318 2326
www.stellamccartney.com

USA
112 Greene Street
New York NY 10014
212-255-1556
www.stellamccartney.com
Saks Fifth Avenue
9600 Wilshire Boulevard
Beverly Hills CA 90212
310-275-4211
www.stellamccartney.com

Saks Fifth Avenue
5800 Glades Road
Boca Raton FL 33431
561-393-9100
www.stellamccartney.com

Temperley London
UK
27 Bruton Street
London W1J 6QN
0207 229 7957
www.temperleylondon.com

2–10 Colville Mews
Lonsdale Road
London W11 2DA
0207 229 7957
www.temperleylondon.com

USA
8452 Melrose Place
West Hollywood CA 90069
323-782-8000
www.temperleylondon.com

Topshop
UK
Brigstowe Street
Bristol BS1 3BA
0117 9294991
www.topshop.com

65–67 New Street
Huddersfield HD1 2BQ
01484 517149
www.topshop.com

36–38 Great Castle Street
London W1W 8LG
0844 8487487
www.topshop.com

USA
830 North Michigan Avenue
Chicago 60611
312-280-6834
www.topshop.com

Topshop Fashion Show Mall
3200 Las Vegas Boulevard South
Las Vegas NV 89109
702-866-0646
www.topshop.com

478 Broadway
New York NY 10013
212-966-9555
www.topshop.com

Australia
500 Chapel Street
South Yarra VIC 3141
61-3-8844-0900
www.topshop.com

Canada
Topshop, Pacific Centre
674 Granville Street
Vancouver BC V6C 1Z6
604-681-6211
www.topshop.com

Twenty8Twelve
UK
8 Slingsby Place
London WC2E 9AB
020 7042 3500
www.twenty8twelve.com

172 Westbourne Grove
London W11 2RW
020 7221 9287
www.twenty8twelve.com

Westfield
London W12 7GF
020 8749 2450
www.twenty8twelve.com

Westfield Stratford City
London E20 1EN
020 8221 1724
www.twenty8twelve.com

Warehouse
UK
19–21 Argyll Street
London W1F 7TR
020 7437 7101
www.warehouse.co.uk

House of Fraser
c/o Army & Navy
45–51 Park Street
Camberley
Surrey GU15 3PG
01276 418 050
www.warehouse.co.uk

Selfridges
400 Oxford Street
London W1A 1AB
08708 377377
www.warehouse.co.uk

Whistles
UK
135–136 Upper Street
London N1 1QP
020 7226 7551
www.whistles.co.uk

3–7 Middle Pavement
Nottingham NG1 7DX
011594 75551
www.whistles.co.uk
John Lewis
10 Downing Street
Cambridge CB2 3DS
01223 361292
www.whistles.co.uk

John Lewis Oxford Street
278–306 Oxford Street
London W1C 1DX
020 7629 7711
www.whistles.co.uk

Zara
UK
118 Regent Street
London W1B 5FE
020 7534 9500
www.zara.com

79–83 Brompton Road
London SW3 1DB
020 7590 6960
www.zara.com

48–52 Kensington High Street
London W8 4PE
020 7368 4680
www.zara.com

USA
212 Newbury Street
Boston MA 02116
617-236-1414
www.zara.com

6902 Hollywood Blvd.
Los Angeles CA 90028
323-469-1002
www.zara.com

689 5th Ave
New York NY 10022
212-371-2555
www.zara.com

Australia
Bourke Street Mall
Melbourne VIC
03-8663-0400
www.zara.com

Westfield Sydney
Sydney NSW
02-9216-7000
www.zara.com

Canada
Chinook Centre
6455 MacLeod Trail SW
Calgary AB T2H OK8
403-538-2357
www.zara.com

Hair

**James Pryce and Richard Ward
at Richard Ward salon**
UK
82 Duke of York Square
London SW3 4LY
020 7730 1222
http://richardward.com

USA
Yarok Beauty Kitchen
39 West 19th Street
New York 10011
212-876-4293
www.yarokhair.com

Jewellery

Accessorize/Monsoon
UK
443 The Strand
London WC2R 0QU
0207 240 7054
www.uk.accessorize.com

Annoushka
UK
41 Cadogan Gardens
London SW3 2TB
020 7881 5828
www.annoushka-jewellery.com

1 South Molton Street
London W1K 5QF
020 7629 8233
www.annoushka-jewellery.com

Bicester Village
50 Pingle Drive
Oxon OX26 6WD
0186 924 9948
www.annoushka-jewellery.com

Azuni
UK John Lewis
300 Oxford Street
London W1A 1EX
020 7629 7711
http://azuni.co.uk

**Buckley Jewellery (Adrian
Buckley)**
Stocked worldwide
www.buckleylondon.com

Cartier
UK
143–144 Sloane Street
London SW1X 9AY
020 7312 6930
www.cartier.co.uk

40–41 Old Bond Street
London W1S 4QR
020 7290 5150
www.cartier.co.uk
Selfridges
400 Oxford Street
London W1A 1AB
020 7318 3977
www.cartier.co.uk

USA
653 Fifth Avenue
New York NY 10022
212-753-0111
www.cartier.co.uk

Eyes on Lincoln
708 Lincoln Road
Miami Beach FL 33139
305-532-0070
www.cartier.co.uk

Saks Fifth Avenue
310 Canal Street
New Orleans LA 70130
504-524-2200
www.cartier.co.uk
Australia
The Moroccan Center
9–11 Elkhorn Avenue
Surfers Paradise
1800-13-0000
www.cartier.co.uk

43 Castlereagh Street
Sydney NSW
1800-13-0000
www.cartier.co.uk

Canada
3401 Dufferin Street
Toronto ON M6A 2T9
416-787-7474
www.cartier.co.uk

Catherine Zoraida
UK
Austique
330 King's Road
London SW3 5UR
020 7376 4555
www.catherinezoraida.com

Felt
13 Cale Street
London SW3 3QS
020 7349 8829
www.catherinezoraida.com

Wolf & Badger
46 Ledbury Road
London W11 2AB
020 7229 5698
www.catherinezoraida.com

Garrard
UK
24 Albemarle Street
London W1S 4HT
0870 871 8888
www.garrard.com

Harvey Nichols
109–125 Knightsbridge
London SW1X 7RJ
020 7235 5000
www.garrard.com

USA
Saks Fifth Avenue
384 Post Street
San Francisco CA 94108
415-986-4300
www.garrard.com

V.A.U.L.T
1024 Lincoln Road
Miami Beach FLA 33139
305-673-5251
www.garrard.com

Heavenly Necklaces
0203 162 3048
www.heavenlynecklaces.com

Kiki McDonough (see
Accessories, page 165)

Links of London
UK
Fenwick
Brent Cross Shopping Centre
London NW4 3FN
020 8732 8285
www.linksoflondon.com

94 Jermyn Street
London SW1Y 6JE
020 7930 0400/0401
www.linksoflondon.com

Westfield
London W12 7GD
020 8749 7774
www.linksoflondon.com

USA
The Mall at Short Hills
115 Short Hills NJ 07078
973-376-0911
www.linksoflondon.com

535 Madison Avenue
New York 10022
212-588-1177
www.linksoflondon.com

Links of London at Bloomingdales
909 North Michigan Avenue
Chicago IL 60611
312-440-4460
www.linksoflondon.com

Canada
Holt Renfrew
Eaton Centre
Calgary T2P 4H9
001-403-269-7341
www.linksoflondon.com

Holt Renfrew
10180 101 Street Northwest
Edmonton AB T5J 3S4
001-780-425-5300
www.linksoflondon.com

Holt Renfrew
Bloor Street
Toronto M4W 1A1
001-416-960-4039
www.linksoflondon.com

Mappin & Webb
UK
132 Regent Street
London W1B 5SF
020 7287 0033
General no: 0800 111 4524
www.mappinandwebb.com

28 Buchanan Street
Glasgow G1 3LB
0141 221 7683

Monica Vinader
UK
Monica Vinader Mayfair Boutique
14 South Molton Street
London W1K 5QP
Tel: +44(0)20 7629 5588
www.monicavinader.com

USA
Monica Vinader NYC Boutique
151 Spring Street, Soho
New York, NY 10012

Tiffany & Co. (Elsa Peretti)
UK
25 Old Bond Street
London W1S 4QB
020 7409 2790
www.tiffany.co.uk

145 Sloane Street
London SW1X 9AY
020 7409 2790
www.tiffany.co.uk
Westfield
London W12 7GQ
020 7409 2790
www.tiffany.co.uk

USA
730 North Michigan Avenue
Chicago, IL 60611
312-944-7500
www.tiffany.com

Fifth Avenue and 57th Street
New York, NY 10022
212-755-8000
www.tiffany.com

5481 Wisconsin Avenue
Chevy Chase, MD 20815
301-657-8777
www.tiffany.com

Australia
226 Queen Street
Brisbane, QLD 4000
1-800-731-131
www.tiffany.com.au

37 King Street
Perth WA 6000
1-800-731-131
www.tiffany.com.au

28 Castlereagh Street
Sydney NSW 2000
1-800-731-131
www.tiffany.com.au

Canada
25 The West Mall
Toronto, ON M9C 1B8
416-695-2112
www.tiffany.ca

3401 Dufferin Street
Toronto, Ontario M6A 2T9
416-780-6570
www.tiffany.ca

37 Dunsmuir Street
Vancouver BC V7Y 1E4
604-235-4111
www.tiffany.ca

Makeup & Fragrances

Bobbi Brown
UK
Browns
34–40 Eastgate Row
Chester
Cheshire CH1 3SB.
01244 403213
www.bobbibrown.co.uk

Elys
16 St Georges Road
London SW19 4DP
020 8946 9191
www.bobbibrown.co.uk

Selfridges & Co.
400 Oxford Street
London W1U 1AT
020 7437 4370
www.bobbibrown.co.uk

USA
Bobbi Brown – The Studio
8 Lackawanna Plaza
Montclair, NJ 07042
973-783-3506
www.bobbibrowncosmetics.com

Dillard's
6000 West Markham
Little Rock AR 72205
501-661-0053
www.bobbibrowncosmetics.com

Sephora
150 Broadway
New York NY 10038
212-566-8600
www.bobbibrowncosmetics.com

Australia
David Jones Claremont Quarters
47–49 Bayview Terrace
Claremont WA 6010
08-9210-5600
www.bobbibrown.com.au

Mecca Maxima Melbourne
GD 54/55 Melbourne Central La
Trobe Building
Melbourne VIC 3000
61-3-9639-5897
www.bobbibrown.com.au

Myer Sydney City
436 George Street
Sydney NSW 2000
61-2-9238-9111
www.bobbibrown.com.au

Illuminum Perfume
UK
41–42 Dover Street
London W1S 4NS
http://illuminumperfume.com

Index

Figures in italics indicate captions.

1950s-style 87

African Cats (film) 82
AG 53
air travel tips 57
Alba, Jessica 46
Albini 37
Alexander McQueen 73, 88, 96, 114, 124: belts *67*; blouses *45*; bridesmaid dress 17; clutch bags 97, 107, 109, 151; coat-dress 155; coats *45*, 155; dresses 42, *42*, 63, 81, 100, 130, 137; skirts *45*; suits 28; wedding dress 6, 8, *24*, 42, 87, 88, 119
Amanda Wakeley Store, Fulham Road, London 64
Andrew, Prince 51
Aniston, Jennifer 60
Anne, Princess, HRH The Princess Royal *15*
Annoushka Jewellery 118
Aquatalia 68, 142, 155
Araki, Nobuyoshi: "Sensual Flowers" 120
ARK (Absolute Return for Kids), Gala for 60, 84
Armani, Giorgio 94
Art Deco 144
As Syakirin Mosque, Kuala Lumpur 127, 128
Asda 100
ASOS Maternity Collection 161
Asprey *17*, 159
Atherton, Amber 130
Aubrey-Fletcher, Harry 13
Audi Polo Challenge, Coworth Park, Berkshire 88
Azuni 139

Bacon's College, southeast London 104
Badminton Horse Trials *11*
BAFTA dinner, Los Angeles 63, 120
Bags: bowling 30; bowling (Prada) 30; "Bristol" (Modalu) 17; Mulberry tiger-print 13; "Polly Push" (Mulberry) 152
see also clutch bags
Banana Republic 30
Barbour wax jackets 11
Beatrice, Princess 38, 142
Beaufort Polo Club *11*
Beckham, Victoria 114, 141

Beckinsale, Kate 67
Bellville Sassoon 91
belt buckles 50, 53, *69*
belts 68, 69, *69*, 98, 114, 158: Alexander McQueen *67*; "Betony" (Reiss) 142, 143; bow 144, 145; essential belt collection 143; Linda Camm 46; Reiss 78
Bennett, Linda Kristin 45
Berney, Douglas 51
Beulah London *79*, 127
Beyoncé 60, 111
Bicester Village Shopping Outlet 12, 73, 142
Black Watch tartan 155
blazers 6, 11, *19*: flared 98; One-Button (Smythe) *46*, 110, 111, 112; the perfect blazer 76; Smythe 48; Zara 74
Blenheim Palace: game fair *11*
blogs 5, 13
blouses: nautical (Alexander McQueen) *45*; Next 17; "Sub Silky Tie Top" (French Connection) 158
Bobbi Brown make-up 31, 128
Boodle Boxing Ball *8*
Boots: "Hi and Dry" (Aquatalia by Marvin K) 68; "Rhumba" (Aquatalia) 142, 155; riding-style 89; "Vegas Setter" (R. Soles) 51; Vierzon wellington (Le Chameau) 70; wellies (Hunter) 11, 89; wellies (Le Chameau) 28
Boots, King's Road, Chelsea 57
Bracelets: Art Deco diamond cluster 144; "C" charm bracelet 58; diamond 63, 120, 151; "Diamonds by the Yard" (Tiffany) 32, 78, 115; fundraising (Imogen Sheeran for EACH) 78, *79*; Links of London 40; "Spread Your Wings" (Catherine Zoraida) 130
Bradby, Claudia 11, 37
British Airways 6
British Armed Forces 151
British Fashion Awards *42*, 107
British Film Institute 82
British Olympic Association 74
British Paralympic Association 74
Brolliesgalore 124
Brooches: dolphin 96; maple-leaf 38; poppy-shaped (Adrian Buckley) 151
Brown, Bobbi 31
Bruni-Sarkozy, Carla 38
Buckingham Palace, London 13, *15*, 94, 107, 144, 152

Buckley, Adrian 151
Burberry 13
Burton, Sarah: coat-dress 155; dresses 42, *42*, 63, 96, 100; wedding dress 6, 8, *24*, 42, 87, 88
buttons 145

Calgary Stampede 50, 53
Cameron, Samantha 32, 93, 101
Camilla, Duchess of Cornwall (Camilla Parker Bowles) 58, 96
Camm, Linda 46
Campbell, Naomi 114
Canada and North America tour *see under* tours
Canada Day concert 38
Capri pants 12
Casino Royale (film) 60
Catherine, Duchess of Cambridge ("Kate"; née Middleton): accessories buyer for Jigsaw 11, 37, 105; awarded History of Art degree 11; insider jokes 73, 112, 114, 149; known as the "thrifty Royal" 73; pregnancy *157*, 158, 159, 161; signature style 6, 11, 64, 89, 141, 161
"Cecile" dress 32
celebrity designers, picking the right 141
Céline 73
Centrepoint, London 68
chain store buys 105
Chanel-style tweed blazer *19*
Chantilly lace 137
Charles, HRH The Prince of Wales 96, 118, 159
Child Bereavement Charity *79*
Chinoiserie 58
Chloé 155
Choo, Jimmy 57
Clarence House, London 124
Closer magazine 134
Cluny lace 137
clutch bags 11, 28, 65, 87: "Charlie" (Wilbur & Gussie) 131; "Classic" (Alexander McQueen) 151; Classic Skull Clutch with Silk Bow (Alexander McQueen) 97; Emmy Scarterfield 82; fan-shaped (Anya Hindmarch) 37; Jenny Packham 86; L.K. Bennett 12, 32; "Maud" (Anya Hindmarch) 38, 115, 120; "Muse" (Russell & Bromley) 111; "Natalie" (L.K. Bennett) 55, *55*, 58, 64, 128; "Park Avenue" (Russell

& Bromley) 117; Prada 93, 101; quilted Jaeger 42; "Somerton" (Hobbs) 40; suede (Alexander McQueen) 107, 109; "Ubai" (Jimmy Choo) 63
coat-dresses 94: Black Watch tartan (Alexander McQueen) 155; Catherine Walker 19, 57; Christopher Kane 107; Emilia Wickstead 93; "Marianne" (Catherine Walker) 96; "Trina" (Reiss) 78, 81
coats: "Angel Fit and Flare" (Reiss) 142, 157; Burberry 13; "Dulwich" (Libélula) 88, 91; Libélula 13; M by Missoni 73; military (Alexander McQueen) *45*; Missoni 12; sheepskin (L.K. Bennett) 28; wool *69*
Cole, Lily 114
Colours: blue 28, 81; pink 93; red 81; teal 12, 84; white 65; yellow 81
Contostavlos, Tulisa 96
Cook Tucker, Amanda 118
Corbett, Jane 94
country casuals 11
country style 89
cowgirl outfits 50–53
Cox, Patrick 89
Cranston, Sophie 88, 91

Daily Mail 15, 104, 158
Darel, Gérard 19
Daunt Books, Chelsea 19
Day-Glo Midnight Roller Disco Charity *24*
de Gournay 58, 117: Eclectic collection 58
Debenhams department store 12, 82
demure glamour 63
Devil Wears Prada, The (film) 15, 60
Diamond Jubilee celebrations 6, 28, 81, 93, 94, 100, 152
Diamond Jubilee Concert 114
Diamond Jubilee tea party, Kuala Lumpur 134
Diamond Jubilee Tour *see under* tours
Diana, Princess of Wales 15, 30, 38, 40, 45, 55, 57, 64, 67, 93, 117, 127, 144, 155, 158
Diaz, Cameron 60
Die Another Day (film) 60
Diesel 53
"diffusion" lines 105
Dior 73
Dorchester hotel, London 139

Dorothy Perkins 141
Dresses: Amanda Wakeley
64; "Amoret" (Temperley
London) 149, *149*;
"Aspen" teal ballgown
(Jenny Packham) 12, 84,
87; "Aster Flower Dress"
(Temperley London) 134;
"Ayden" (Roksanda Ilincic)
19; "Beatrice" (Temperley
London) *147*; "Bella"
(Whistles) 114, 115;
block (Paper London) 17;
"Blossom" (Beulah London)
127; bridesmaid (Alexander
McQueen) 17, *24*; "Cecile"
(Erdem Moralioglu) 32;
chiffon (Temperley London)
147; embroidered black
(Temperley London) 144,
145; emerald 94; Erdem
28; "Esmeralda" (Temperley
London) 144; evening
gown (Alice Temperley) 28;
floor-length (Issa) *8*; floral
(Jenny Packham) *8*, 28,
58; floral (Prabal Gurung)
28, 120; "Forever" (Issa)
17; gold lamé-embroidered
(Alexander McQueen) 130,
131, 132; Grecian-style
(Alexander McQueen)
63; Grecian-style (Jenny
Packham) 60; Grecian-style
evening gown 67; Issa
13, 30, 38; "Kensington"
(Catherine Walker) 40;
kimono-style (Jenny
Packham) 117; "Moriah"
(Temperley London) *147*;
"Nannette" (Reiss) 13, 35,
35, 65; "Penelope" (Project
D) 139; "Peridot" (Roksanda
Ilincic) 55; "Phoebe Bluebird
Peplum" (Project D) 139;
"Rebecca" (Libélula) 88;
Reiss 12; "Ridley Stretch
Cady" (Stella McCartney)
110, 112; "Sabriti" (Beulah
London) 127; sailor 42, *42*,
65; "Sarai" evening gown
(Beulah London) *79*; scarlet
(Alexander McQueen) 81, 96,
157; sequinned gown (Jenny
Packham) 60; shift *132*; shift
(Alexander McQueen) 100,
137; shift (Phase Eight) 17;
"Shola" bandage (Reiss) 13,
15; "Sofie Rae" (Whistles)
158, 159; Stella McCartney
19; summer (Hobbs) 104;
sweater – glamming up
69; sweater (Alexander
McQueen) 42; sweater

(Ralph Lauren Blue Label)
68; transparent (Charlotte
Todd) 8, *22*, 149; "Vespa"
patchwork (Paper London)
19; wedding (Alexander
McQueen) 6, 8, *24*, 42, 87,
88, 119; wrap-dress 30, 31,
38; Zara 13
Ducas, Annoushka 118
Dundas, Peter 74

Earrings: amazonite (Azuni)
139; blue topaz and diamond
(Kiki McDonough) 109, 114;
citrine and diamond (Kiki
McDonough) 143; citrine
drop (Kiki McDonough)
58; "Classic Baroque Pearl
Earring Drops" (Annoushka
Jewellery) 118, *151*; cubic
zirconia 101; diamanté 86,
87; diamond 135, 151;
diamond chandelier 63;
diamond and sapphire 45,
155, 158; "Double Leaf"
(Catherine Zoraida) 130;
drop 32; "Grace" (Kiki
McDonough) 55, 65; "Hope
Egg" (Links of London) 40,
73; "Kiki Classic" 82; white
topaz and diamond (Kiki
McDonough) 69
East Anglia's Children's
Hospices (EACH) 78, *79*
Edward, Prince 51
elbow patches 145
Elizabeth, Queen, the Queen
Mother 38
Elizabeth II, Queen 12, 28, 37,
38, 63, 73, 94, 96, 100, 123
Emmy Shoes 82
Emsley, Paul 158
engagement ring 30, 32, 45,
65
Episode 78, 159
Epsom Derby 12, 64
Erdem 28, 114, 137
Eugenie, Princess 38, 100, 142
eyebrows 128

Facebook 13
fascinators 13, 37, 98, 101:
Whiteley Hat Company 12
fashion choices 112
Fawcett, Farrah 152
Ferragamo, Salvatore 30, 31
Fletcher, Sylvia 37, 97, 98
florals: how to wear without
looking frumpy 59
Fortnum & Mason 73
Foyles bookstore, London 19
French Connection 158
French Sole 37

Gap 161
Garrard 30
George at Asda 13, 20, 74
Go Silk, New York 67
Golden Metropolitan Polo Club
Charity Cup polo match *11*
Goldschmied, Adriano 53
Goldsign 53
Goodwin, Dr Harold 15
graphic prints 120, 121
Greatest Team Rises Olympic
gala event 84
Greenwich Village 142
Gucci 73
Gurung, Prabal 28, 120

H&M 105
Hadden, Belinda 101
hair stylist 37, 118
hairpins 135
hairstyles: blow-dried 12,
31, 84; chignon 39, 84,
135; and formal hats 102;
loosely pinned back 57,
132; perfectly in place 104;
ponytail 42; retro look 152,
153
Halim, Sultan Abdul 130
Hall, Jerry 88
Harper's Bazaar: crowns Kate
"Queen of Style" 8
Harry, Prince *11*, 96, 104, 118
Hathaway, Anne 15
hats: beret-style cap (Sylvia
Fletcher) 37, 97; cocktail
102; cocktail (Jane Taylor)
100; cocktail (Sylvia
Fletcher) 97, 98; Jane
Corbett 94; Lock & Co. 94;
safari-style 71; Stetson
(Smithbilt Hats Inc.) 50–51;
wear formal hats with flair
102
Heavenly Necklaces 101
Helayel, Daniella Issa 38
Hepburn, Audrey 12
Hicks, India 93
Hindmarch, Anya 37, 93, 115,
120: Bespoke collection 38
Hobbs 40, 104, 105
Holland, Sam 17
Hollie de Keyser boutique,
London 13
Hollywood 13, 15, 63, 87, 141
Holmes, Katie 46
Hook, Camilla 17
House of Fraser 78, 159
Hunter 11, 89
Hurley, Elizabeth 117

Ilincic, Roksanda 19, 55
Illuminum 40
Imperial War Museum
Foundation *67*

In Kind Direct charity
reception *67*
Irish Guards 94
Isaacs, Lady Natasha Rufus
127
Isabella Oliver 161
Issa *8*, 13, 17, 30, 38, 73
Istana Negara Palace, Kuala
Lumpur *132*
Ivy restaurant, London 139

J Brand 46, *46*, 48, 74, 105
Jackets: Barbour wax 11;
Joseph 12; Punto Milano
(Pucci) 74; shearling
"Darwin" (L.K. Bennett) 70;
Zara 17
Jacobs, Marc 89
Jaeger 42, *79*, 81, 124
jeans *19*, 28, 89: coral 74;
J Brand 48, 105; J Brand
811 "Olympia" 46, *46*, 48;
maternity 161; "Passion"
boot-cut (Goldsign) 53; "Pop
Slim Fit" (Zara) 74; Straight
(Twenty8Twelve) 70
Jenny Packham London 60
jewellery 32, 37
Jigsaw high-street store 11, 37,
105: "Junior" range 20
Jimmy Choo 63, 86, 131, 144,
149, 152: 24:7 collection 57
Johansson, Scarlett 37, 38, 67
John Lewis 17, 139
Jolie, Angelina 37, 111, 117
Joseph 12
Jubilee Service of Thanksgiving
100, 101

Kane, Christopher 107
Kardashian, Kim 96
Kardashian sisters 141
"Kate Effect" 8, 13, 15, 64, 73,
91, 101, 114
Kate Spade New York 17
Kate's Style List (mobile app)
13
Kelly, Grace 87
Keys, Abbey 130–31
King's Road, Chelsea *19*, 30,
51, 57
Klosters, Switzerland *22*
Knightley, Keira 60
Kors, Michael 155
Kranji War Memorial, Singapore
123–24

Lace, how to wear 137
Lagerfeld, Karl 20, 105
Lambert, Fiona 20, 74, 100
Laura Ashley 89
Lauren, Ralph 155
Le Caprice restaurant, London
139

Le Chameau 28, 70–71, 89
Leicester, Diamond Jubilee visit
    to 159
Libélula 13, 88, 91
Links of London 40, 73, 118
L.K. Bennett: bags 55, *55*, 64,
    128; coats 28, 70; shoes 13,
    32, 45, 48, *60*, 64, 97, 101,
    104, 123, 128, 135, 139;
    Signature collection 58, 70
LLC Ltd 71
local style 53
Lock & Co., James 37, 94, 97
London 2012 Olympic Games 6,
    15, *15*, *24*, *46*, 74, 84, 104,
    110, 111, 112, 114, 115
London 2012 Paralympics 76
London Designer Show 60
Lupfer, Markus 19
Lyons, Lucy 131

McCartney, Stella 19, 96, 107,
    110, 112
McDonough, Kiki 55, 58, 65,
    69, 82, 109, 114, 143
McQueen, Alexander 91
Madame Tussauds, London 63
Mahiki nightclub *22*
make-up: Bobbi Brown 31;
    eye *135*; eyeshadow powder
    (Bobbi Brown) 128; muted
    tones 31; perfect occasion
    83; signature 86
Manolo Blahniks 13
Marshall, Ashley 139
Marvin K (Marvin Krasnow) 68
Middleton, Carole 19, *19*, 20,
    40, 78, 83
Middleton, Pippa 17, *17*,
    19, 131, 134, 139, 144:
    Celebrate: A Year of British
    Festivities for Families and
    Friends 17, 19
Miller, Savannah 70
Miller, Sienna 37, 70, 127
Minogue, Dannii 93, 139, 141
Mirren, Helen 67
Missoni 12, 73, 105
Missoni, Angela 73
Missoni, Tai and Rosita 73
Miu Miu 73
mobile apps 13
Modalu 17
Monroe, Marilyn 30
Montefiore, Simon Sebag:
    Young Stalin 17
Montgomery, Lucy Maud: *Anne*
    of Green Gables 42
Moore, Demi 67, 127
Moralioglu, Erdem 32: Resort
    2012 collection 32
Moss, Kate 30, 38, 114, 127
Mulberry 13, 73: "Peace and
    Love" jacquard design 152

Mulligan, Carey 30
Murray, Andy 110
myflashtrash.com 130
Nails 83
National Memorial Arboretum
    Appeal 60
National Portrait Gallery,
    London 110, 158
Natural History Museum,
    London: "Treasures"
    exhibition 152
nautical look 42, *42*, *45*
Naysmith, Christine 124
Naysmith, Linda 124
necklaces 87: Asprey 167
    Button Pendant 159;
    "Cabochon by the Yard" (Elsa
    Peretti) 32, 78; "coffee bean"
    11; Links of London 40
Nenshi, Naheed 51
"new demure, the" 12
New York Fashion Week 120
Newcastle Civic Centre *69*
Next 17
Next.com 74
Nivea Visage Pure & Natural
    Moisturising Day Cream 57

Obama, Barack 13, 38
Obama, Michelle 13, *15*, 32,
    38, 55, 107, 120
Olympic medalists' reception,
    Buckingham palace 144
Onassis, Jackie 74
O'Regan, Marie 100

Packham, Jenny *8*, 12, 58, 60,
    60, 84, 86, 87, 117, 123,
    124
Paltrow, Gwyneth 32, 55
pants: see trousers
pantyhose 128
Paper London 17, 19
Paralympics GB 84
parasol 124
Parker, Sarah Jessica 120,
    127
Parker Bowles, Emma 93
Party Pieces mail-order
    company 20
pendant, diamond-studded
    silver cross 65
Peretti, Elsa 32, 78
Peron, Eva 30
Phase Eight 17
Philip, HRH Prince, Duke of
    Edinburgh 51, 64, 96, *123*
Phillips, Zara 64, 100
Pied à Terre 104
"Pippa Effect" 17
pleats 124, 151
Prada 30, 38, 73, 93, 101, 120
Pregnancy: how to dress your
    bump 159; maternity wear

    161
Project D 139, *139*, 141
Pucci 74, 76
R. Soles 51
Rainier, Prince, of Monaco 87
Ralph Lauren Blue Label 68
Redgrave, Sir Steve *15*
Reiss 12, 13, *15*, 35, *35*, 78,
    117, 142
Reiss, David 13
Remembrance Day 151
retro chic 152
Richard Ward Hair Salon,
    Chelsea 37, 84, 118, 152,
    153
RN Submarine Service 96
Rodriguez, Narciso 94
Rothchild, Judy 51
Royal Air Force 151
Royal British Legion 151
Royal Family 11, 51, 63, 78,
    81, 94, 96, 100
Royal Foundation 104
Royal Garden Parties 94
Royal Lancaster Hotel, London
    8
Royal Marsden Hospital, Sutton,
    Surrey 64
Royal Wedding 17, 19, 20,
    40, 88
Russell & Bromley 68, 111, 117

St Andrew's Day 155
St Andrew's preparatory school,
    Pangbourne, Berkshire 155,
    157, *157*
St David's Day 28, 73, 112
St George's Park National
    Football Centre, Staffordshire
    142
St Giles Cathedral, Edinburgh
    94
St James's Palace, London: ARK
    children's charity gala *60*, 84
St Patrick's Day 93, 94
St Paul's Cathedral 100, 101
Sanderson, Rupert 73
Santa Barbara Polo & Racquet
    Club: charity polo match
    8, 58
satin: wearing it in style 109
Saudi Arabia, Crown Prince
    of 45
Scarterfield, Emmy 82
scarves 96: headscarf (Beulah
    London) 127, 128
scent: White Gardenia Petals
    (Illuminum) 40
Scherzinger, Nicole 46
Schouler, Proenza 94
Sebago 48
sense of occasion 119
Séraphine 161
sheer fabrics 151

Sheeran, Ed 78, *79*
Sheeran, Imogen 78, *79*
Shepherdson, Jane 114
shirt: "Rodeo" (Temperley
    London) 50
shirt dresses: "Full Pleated
    Shirt Dress" (Mulberry)
    152; Jaeger *79*, 81; Jenny
    Packham 123
shoes: "Angel" (Episode)
    78, 1569; ballet flats 12,
    37; "Coco Pops" (Stuart
    Weitzman) 111; "Cosmic"
    pumps (Jimmy Choo) 144,
    149, 152; court 11, 37,
    63, 98; court (L.K.Bennett)
    45; "Dart Glitter" sandals
    (Jimmy Choo) 131; "Dela"
    pumps (Tabitha Simmons)
    40; "Imperia" wedges (Pied
    à Terre) 104; kitten heels
    (Ferragamo) 30, 31; "Lovely"
    stilettos 57; "Maddox"
    wedges 48; "Malone" pumps
    (Rupert Sanderson) 73;
    "Minx" espadrilles (Stuart
    Weitzman) 88; nude 6,
    32, 64, 65, 81, 117; "Park
    Avenue" pumps (Russell &
    Bromley) 117–18; pointed-
    toed (Ferragamo) 30; Prada
    heels 38, 120; pumps 40;
    pumps (L.K. Bennett) 13;
    pumps (Prada) 93; "Sandy"
    sandal (L.K. Bennett) 58;
    Sebago "Bala" deck shoes
    48; "Sledge" pumps (L.K.
    Bennett) 32, 64, 97, 101,
    104, 123, 128, 135, 139;
    "Valerie" pumps (Emmy
    Scarterfield) 82; "Vamp"
    sandals (Jimmy Choo) 63,
    86; wedges 48, 88, 89, 98
shopping: stay unruffled as you
    shop 31
show-stopping outfits 132
Simmons, Tabitha 40
Singapore Botanical Gardens
    117, 118, 119
Sisterhood rowing team *22*
skincare 83
skirts: choosing skirt shapes
    98; pencil 76; pencil
    (Alexander McQueen) *45*
Skyfall (film) 67
Sloane Rangers 11
"Sloane" style 11
Smith, Jada Pinkett 67
Smithbilt Hats Inc. 50
Smythe Les Vestes *46*, 48, 110
Sophie, Countess of Wessex
    100
Sovereign's Parade, Royal
    Military Academy, Sandhurst

20
Spagnoli, Luisa 13
Spencer, Lady Kitty 93
Spielberg, Steven 149
Spirit of Chartwell (royal barge)
  96
Spirit of Christmas Shopping
  festival, Olympia exhibition
  hall, London *19*
sport supporters 71
Starlight Children's foundation
  8
Stefani, Gwen 12
Stock Exchange, The,
  Bucklebury, Berkshire 73
Stourton, Sarah 13
Strathearn, Countess of 96,
  157
Strathearn tartan 96
Strong, Sir Roy 94
style tricks 115
suits: Amanda Wakeley 67;
  Gérard Darel 19; Luisa
  Spagnoli 13; scarlet
  (Alexander McQueen) 28
sunglasses: Givenchy SGV
  761 111
Swarovski crystals *60*, 84
sweater: turtleneck
  "Honeycomb Tunic" (Alice
  Temperley) 70

Tartan 96, 155, 157, *157*
Taylor, Jane 100–101
Team GB 74, 84, 110
tee shirts 74
Teenage Cancer Trust
  Christmas Spectacular *147*
Temperley, Alice 28, 50, 70, 91,
  105, 134–35, 144, 149
Temperley London 50, 65, 88,
  91, 134, 137, 144, 145, *147*,
  149, *149*
Tesco 13
Testino, Mario 13, 73
Thames Diamond Jubilee River
  Pageant 81, 96, 98, 151, 157
Theron, Charlize 67
Thistle Ceremony, Edinburgh
  94, 157
Tiffany 32, 78, 115
Time magazine 8, 17, *42*
Todd, Charlotte 8, *22*, 149
Top Shop Maternity 161
Tours: Canada and North
  America (2011) 28, 32, 35,
  37, 40, 42, 46, *46*, 50, 64,
  65, 96, 97, 128, *151*, 152;
  Diamond Jubilee Tour (2012)
  24, 57, *79*, 81, 117, 118,
  127, 130, 134, 139, *147*
Treehouse children's hospice,
  Ipswich, The 78
Trilogy Stores, Chelsea 53

trousers: Capri 12; cargo (J
  Brand "Houlihan") 46; JBrand
  "Love Story" flares 46
Tusk Trust 82
tweed 89
Twenty8Twelve 70
Twitter 6, 13, 120
Tyne, Brett 131

UK Jewellery Awards 151
understated elegance 100
underwear, and satin 109
UNICEF 158
University of St Andrews 11,
  13, *22*, 37, 71: Fashion Show
  8, *22*, 149
US Open Tennis Championships
  17

Vanda William Catherine orchid
  117, 119
visible panty line (VPL) 109,
  137
Vogue magazine 28, 91, 94

Wakeley, Amanda 64, 67, *67*
Waktare, Karl 71
Walker, Catherine 19, 40, 57
wallpaper: "Windswept
  Blossom" (de Gournay) 58
War Horse (film) 149, *149*, 151
Warehouse 30, 105
Watson, Emma 88
Webb, Tabitha Somerset 139
Weitzman, Stuart 88, 111
Westminster Abbey, London 17
Weymouth: Women's Laser
  Radial race *15*
What Kate Wore (blog) 13
Whistles 12, 30, 114, 158
Whiteley Hat Company 12
Wickstead, Emilia 93, 94
Wilbur & Gussie 131
William, Prince 8, 11, *11*, 17,
  28, 30, 40, 45, 46, *46*, 50–
  51, *60*, 68, *79*, 82, 84, 88,
  93, 104, 110, 117, 118, 139,
  139, 143, 144, 149, 151,
  151, 157, 158
Williamson, Matthew 82, 107:
  bridal gowns 82; Butterfly by
  Matthew Williamson 82; MW
  Matthew Williamson 82
Wimbledon *24*, 42, 110, *147*
Winslet, Kate 67, 117
World Sovereign's lunch,
  Windsor Castle 93

Yeomans, Lucy 8
York, Duchess of 38

Zara 13, 17, 74, 105
Zoraida, Catherine 130

Acknowledgements

The publishers would like to thank the following sources for their kind permission to reproduce the pictures in this book.
Key: t=Top, b=Bottom, c=Centre, l=Left and r=Right
Annoushka Jewellery: 118cr, 195 (Pearl earring drops)
Anya Hindmarch: 38r, 195c (Black silk 'Maud' clutch bag)
Bear Holding Ltd: 71
Beulah London: /www.beulahlondon.com: 127
Catherine Zoraida: /www.catherinezoraida.com: 130r, 195c ('Spread your wings' gold bracelet)
Corbis: /Mike Nelson/epa: 7
Images Courtesy East Anglia's Children's Hospices: 79t, 79b,195c (Bracelet - The EACH Bracelet, exclusively designed by Imogen Sheeran, is priced at £10 and is available to buy online at www.each.org.uk/bracelet)
Emmy Shoes: /www.emmyshoes.co.uk: 83r
Getty Images: 1, 4, 9, 11, 23br, 25r, 29br, 33br, 34, 47, 48t, 51r, 52, 65b, 66, 67, 94, 95l, 96, 98, 100, 101r, 102, 103, 110, 111tr, 117b, 117b, 133, 134r, 135, 136, 137, 144, 144b, 148, 149, 150tr, 150bl, 150br, 153, 160bl,162, 164, 167, 168, 170, 171, 172, 174, 175, 176, 191, 192b, 192, 193, 208 /2011 100 Women In Hedge Funds: 80, /2012 Indigo: 88t, /AFP: 14, 23tl, 23tr, 39, 41tr, 45l, 45r, 72l, 74, 75, 77, 84, 106, 113, 123l, 125, 138, 140, /FilmMagic: 20-21, 72br, /UK Press: 10l, 19, 89, 146l, 152, 160tc, /WireImage: 29tl, 29tcl, 29bc, 29bcr, 33l, 33tr, 36tr, 36br, 37, 41l, 44, 46, 48b, 49, 54l, 54r, 58, 65c, 78, 120l, 120r, 123r, 142, 146r, 161, 195c (Red hat)
Heavenly Necklaces: 101l, 194tl
Jimmy Choo: 57, 63, 131l, 194cl, 194br
Kiki McDonough: 59tr, 68r, 115, 195c (Citrine drop earrings, Blue topaz and diamond earrings & White topaz and diamond stud earrings)
L.K. Bennett: 55, 195c ('Natalie' natural clutch bag)
Libélula: 88c, 91
Next Plc: 76
Press Association Images: /Lefteris Pitarakus/PA Archive: 61
Profile: /Illuminum: 40
R. Soles: 50r, 195c (Vegas Setter boots)
Reiss: 35
REX/Shutterstock: 10r, 12, 15, 16, 17, 18, 23tc, 23bl, 26-27, 38l, 50l, 62, 64, 85l, 87, 92, 95r, 114, 131tr, 131br, 134l, 147, 154, 156, 195l, /Ben Cawthra: 97l, 97tr, 97br, 99, /Malcolm Clarke/Daily Mail: 22r, /Davidson/O'Neill: 8, /Paul Grover: 104, 158, /David Hartley/Rupert Hartley: 68l, 69t, 83l, 85r, 86br, 195r, /Ikon Pictures/Niraj Tanna: 90, /Nils Jorgensen: 72tr, 159, /Keystone USA-Zuma: 43, 51l, /Eddie Mulholland: 150tl, /NTI Media Ltd: 70, /Newspix: 141, /Niviere-Chamussy/Sipa: 107, 108, 109, /Dominic O'Neill: 24l, /Tim Rooke: 24r, 56, 59tl, 59b, 60, 65t, 81, 86tl, 86tr, 86bl, 112, 116, 119, 121, 122, 126, 129, 130l, 169, /Rotello/MCP: 13, /Ray Tang/LNP: 180; /Richard Young: 29tr, 82
Russell and Bromley: 69b, 111br, 118tl, 118br, 194bl,195c ('Park Avenue' clutch bag and matching court shoes)
Seraphine: 160tl, 160r,160cb
Stuart Weitzman: 86b, 111bl, 195c, ('Coco Pop' navy shoes)

Every effort has been made to acknowledge correctly and contact the source and/or copyright holder of each picture and Carlton Books Limited apologises for any unintentional errors or omissions, which will be, corrected in future editions of this book.